SHAMANS
AND
KUSHTAKAS

NORTH COAST TALES OF THE SUPERNATURAL

MARY GIRAUDO BECK

ILLUSTRATED BY MARVIN OLIVER

Alaska Northwest Books™
Anchorage • Seattle • Portland

To my husband George
Marge and George senior
my children Doug, Steve, Katy
and my sister Kay

In memory of my brothers
Louis, Ernie, and Mike

Third printing 1994

Library of Congress Cataloging-in-Publication Data
  Beck, Mary Giraudo, 1924–
    Shamans and kushtakas: north coast tales of the supernatural / by Mary Giraudo Beck; illustrated by Marvin Oliver.
    p. cm.
  Includes bibliographical references.
  ISBN 0-88240-406-7
  1. Tlingit Indians—Legends.   2. Haida Indians—Legends.
3. Tlingit Indians—Religion and mythology.   4. Haida Indians—
Religion and mythology.   I. Title.
E99.T6B44   1991   90-1295
398.2'089972—dc20   CIP

Edited by Lorna Price
Cover and book design by Elizabeth Watson
Illustrations by Marvin Oliver

Alaska Northwest Books™
An imprint of Graphic Arts Center Publishing Company
Editorial office: 2208 NW Market Street, Suite 300, Seattle, WA 98107
Catalog and order dept.: P.O. Box 10306, Portland, OR 97210
  800-452-3032

Printed on recycled paper in the United States of America

CONTENTS

ACKNOWLEDGMENTS

The stories included in this work, like those in *Heroes and Heroines in Tlingit–Haida Legend*, have been repeated to me by various Tlingit and Haida friends and students over the forty years I have lived in Ketchikan. Often the tellers related only parts of the stories, or the same stories would be repeated with varying details and outcomes. Therefore, as a guide to retelling the basic story, I made use of several written sources, at the same time weaving in details or outcomes from oral sources. Most frequently used written sources were: Marius Barbeau's *Medicine Men on the North Pacific Coast* (1953); Viola Garfield and Linn Forrest's *The Wolf and the Raven: Totem Poles of Southeast Alaska* (1956); Aurel Krause's *The Tlingit Indians* (1956); Frederica de Laguna's *Under Mount St. Elias: The History and Culture of the Yakutat Indians* (1927); and John Swanton's *Haida Texts and Myths* (1905) and *Tlingit Myths and Texts* (1909).

Although I am unable to name all those who have told me stories over the years, I offer them my deepest appreciation. I would like to thank those who have helped me in recent years: Gil McLeod, Robert and Ivy Peratrovich, Esther Shea, and Elnore Corbett.

Finally, my special thanks go also to Dolly Jensen and Nancy and Jonathan DeWitt for reading the stories for authenticity, and to Lorna Price for her thoroughness and thoughtful concern in dealing with the text.

M. G. B.

PREFACE

The Tlingit and Haida are the Native Americans who inhabit Southeast Alaska, the panhandle that extends from Yakutat at the north end to Ketchikan at the south. While the Tlingit populate all of Southeast, the Haida have established settlements only on the lower half of Prince of Wales Island, west of Ketchikan — the land closest to the northern tip of Vancouver Island, from which they migrated 300 years ago. Living in such proximity naturally led to exchange of ideas and intermarriage, and eventually to the sharing of concepts and legends as well as social structure and practice.

The heroic or wondrous achievements in these tales were used as models for emulation, and the failures as admonitions, by the grandmother of the family to instruct her charges in proper behavior. For she had the duty of transmitting culture, traditions, and customs to the children, while the mother's eldest brother and sister saw to their training in work skills. Both Tlingit and Haida societies were divided into two groups, or phratries, the Raven and the Eagle, and were matrilineal. Membership in a phratry was determined from the mother's line, as were family relationships. Marriage within the phratry was forbidden; an Eagle always married a Raven, and vice versa.

At about eight years of age, a boy went to live with his uncle to learn fishing, hunting, boatbuilding, boating skills, and the proper way to conduct himself as a man. The aunt oversaw the girl's upbringing, teaching her household skills and the manners and conduct befitting a young woman, such as listening quietly while men did the speaking and eating small amounts of food in a dainty manner. When the young girl went into seclusion at puberty, her aunt also made sure that she remained in the screened section of the house, seeing and talking only to her, her mother, or a servant, and then only about necessities and instruction for marriage and for wifely duties. The aunt also chaperoned the girl from the time of her seclusion until her marriage, which followed shortly after this period of withdrawal ended. High-caste girls especially were kept from seeing or talking to young men during this time. Marriages for both the young man and the young woman were arranged by the aunt and the uncle on each side.

As tales of wonder and sometimes magic, these stories appeal to readers of various cultures. Their purpose, however, was not only to amuse the listeners but also to dramatize the values and traditions of their society. While undergoing amazing experiences, the characters, in story after story, display traits that the members of the tribe or clan must possess to maintain its integrity and the pitfalls they must avoid to prevent disintegration. The appearance again and again of the same types of characters in familiar activities, as well as the frequent retelling of the stories, provided a unifying force in the community.

Mary Giraudo Beck
Ketchikan, July 1990

INTRODUCTION

Shaman and kushtaka! Both struck terror in the hearts of the Tlingit and Harda people, for both possessed frightening supernatural powers. The shaman, healer and seer, battled the kushtaka (Tlingit for Land Otter Man; in Haida, gageets) for the spirit of a man in danger of drowning or dying of exposure. Stories of kushtaka exploits, though they may no longer evoke the spine-tingling chill of earlier times, still have the power to mesmerize those who hear them.

The Tlingit and Haida universe abounded with spirits, the essences of things animate and inanimate that possessed powers to heal, supply food sources, and maintain harmony with nature. Clouds, mountains, lakes and rivers, trees and plants, birds, fish, and animals — all possessed spirits that had to be supplicated or appeased.

In this world, boundaries between the animal and human realms were blurred. The early Tlingit or Haida could hear an omen in the hoot of an owl, or a chilling curfew in the croak of a raven. The land otter, as at home in the water as on land, could conjure in their minds a fearful hybrid being of the spirit world.

The chief spirit was Raven, a trickster, shape-changer, and transformer, who organized the world into its present state, changing some inanimate objects into animate beings, endowing men and animals with particular attributes and roles, gaining for all the blessings of water, fire, and the sun, moon, and stars.

The shaman mediated between this spirit world and the human realm. He was a figure of great power in most Native American cultures. Usually male but occasionally female, the shaman either was "called" to his role or inherited the gift from a shaman uncle. Through fasting, ritual, and isolation, the shaman put himself in touch with the spirits of the world, became aware of his own failings, and asked the spirits' help in bringing his life into accord with nature.

The shaman's ceremonial regalia was important. He wore a tunic soaked in seal oil and a necklace of animal claws and amulets. His hair was tied in a topknot, as it grew very long, sometimes almost to the ground. Believed to be the source of his power, his hair was never cut or even combed. For healing ceremonies he often wore a blanket, a necklace of bone "head-scratcher" ornaments, and a bone stuck through the topknot of his hair. But if the ceremony required him to be unclothed, the shaman's hair would be loosened to hang down around his body. His face was blackened with charcoal. He carried an oval rattle and sometimes a hollow bone for blowing away disease, or a soul-catcher, an ivory tube carved with a whale's head at each end, for capturing a departing spirit.

To treat illness, believed to be caused by an evil within the body, arising from thoughts and behavior in conflict with nature, the shaman called upon his spirit powers to draw out the offending matter and heal the patient. The Tlingit and Haida shaman was also a clairvoyant, endowed with special skills and sensitivity. Before raiding parties, his advice was sought on the weather outlook and the chances of victory. If a patient should die, the shaman was able to tell which newborn child would receive the dead person's spirit. His extrasensory powers helped him ferret out witches and enabled him to "find" those lost in the woods or at sea as well as those "saved" by the Land Otter People.

This power did not come without risk. The shaman

was always in danger of losing his identity or of being possessed by the spirit whose power he sought. Therefore, a good shaman renewed his spiritual disciplines and contacts periodically in order to avoid becoming complacent and lax in practice.

Kushtakas were human beings who had been transformed by land otters into creatures similar to themselves, but who retained some human qualities. They kidnapped children, frightened women, and caused storms, avalanches, disease, and famine. Kushtakas had been given their dual role by Raven, when he bestowed on land otters the gifts of being able to live both on land and under water as well as powers of illusion and disguise. In addition, he gave them the special mission of saving those lost at sea or in the woods and transforming them into half-human, half-otter beings like themselves.

The Land Otters fulfilled their mission so well that people suspected them of actively luring victims to their kingdom. Deathly afraid of the animals, humans did not hunt them for food or clothing. Children were taught to beware of the Land Otter People, who would appear as their close relatives to invite them into boats or kidnap them in the woods. They were trained early to resist kushtaka influence by developing a strong will and respecting and observing tribal customs.

One of the shaman's chief roles was to rescue people from the control of the kushtakas through a ritual in which he called upon his spirit powers, foremost of which was the land otter spirit. The first human being to gain possession of this spirit received it directly from the Land Otter chief, but from that time on, an aspiring shaman took possession of this spirit from the land otter itself. First, however, he had

9

to develop strength of mind and body through strict adherence to the daily ritual of bathing in icy waters, exercising, and drinking the juice of the devil's club (*Oplopanax horridus*, a very spiny native ginseng species). Bathing and drinking the purgative juice assured the cleanliness required for attracting the spirit. He had also to acquire other shamanic skills through apprenticeship to a master.

When the aspirant felt ready to receive spirit powers, he entered the woods with only an assistant, to fast and meditate. After eight days, a deserving aspirant would fall into a trance and have a vision, sometimes even losing consciousness. Then he would feel the surge of spirit powers within him and hear their urgent messages, his repetition of their revelations being understandable only to his assistant, who had fasted with him. Once the aspirant became fully conscious again, he and his assistant would search out a land otter, confronting it with a steady stare until it was mesmerized. Then he would cut off part of the otter's tongue, wrap it in a piece of his clothing, and keep it as an amulet, the source of his land otter power.

The shaman's extraordinary powers made him the proper adversary for the kushtaka. To bolster the kushtaka victim's strength of will, the shaman was often sought to call upon his spirit power to prevent the departing spirit of a drowning man from entering an otter-likeness. The shaman's struggle with the kushtakas for the spirit of the Tlingit or Haida became as compelling as the angels' struggle with the devil for the soul of a Christian. But the Tlingit and Haida were not concerned with a non-earthly existence. If captured by land otters, the spirit of the deceased wandered the familiar, earthly world aimlessly, doing mischief like these animals. But the victim rescued by the shaman either returned to his normal life or, if he died, perpetuated himself in a meaningful existence within the makeup of another human being.

In these stories, instances of the benevolence of kushtakas suggest a duality in their nature to match their physical traits. A certain ambiguity also resides in the perception of the physical nature of these mythic creatures. Ordinarily they can't be seen at all, but sometimes kushtakas reveal themselves in elusive shadowy forms; sometimes they are only heard; sometimes the contaminated victim experiences their reality in the furriness of his own arms and legs when he is starting to become a kushtaka himself.

Kushtakas, with their power of illusion, appear in the guise of dead relatives. They take their victims to underground dens that look like proper homes. One victim sees them as hybrid half-human, half-otter beings; another sees their upper lips caught up under their noses to resemble a land otter's mouth, their arms seeming to grow out of their chests rather than their shoulders.

Human beings had some defenses against kushtakas, however. Human blood could erase their human shapes, and urine eradicated kushtaka defilement. Metal also kept them away; nails and even guns warded them off.

These stories, like all Tlingit and Haida myths, were recorded and passed on through storytelling, songs, dances, painting, weaving, and carving. In addition to being told at group gatherings, legends were carved on totem poles and exhibited with pride as a record of family crests and stories.

The literature of the Tlingit and Haida is a powerful mix of history, legend, and myth — the stuff of epics. *Shamans and Kushtakas* presents the exploits of characters who compete for constructive or destructive ends. Of the four stories dealing with men's interaction with kushtakas, three reveal the shaman acting on behalf of men in typical conflict with them. A fourth shows kushtakas in the unusual role of benefactor. Two deal with the revelations by shamans to chosen people of the powers of certain plants. The three remaining stories involve the wrongful use of shamanic power, or witchcraft.

Though these are cautionary tales, the outcome of right or wrong behavior is not always what might be expected. In fact the apparently ambiguous attitude toward good and bad adds a wonderful complexity to the stories. Many of the characters must undertake some form of the classic journey, beset by dangers, challenges, and the sacrifices that heroes are often called upon to make for personal or communal benefit.

Western literature abounds with figures who return from a journey and through their ordeal arrive at a revelation that benefits themselves and society. In the real world, too, we make our journeys for personal or common gains. Journeys, like the Tlingit and Haida heroes' sea voyages, gain knowledge for society; for us, mountain-climbing or weekend retreats, like a shaman's sojourn into the woods, yield self-knowledge. Like the Tlingit or Haida youths readying themselves through tribal ritual for any feat of will or body, we too test ourselves in the search for perpetually elusive truths. Transcending time and culture, the metaphor of the journey envisions man's constant struggle to understand and experience the mysteries of the universe.

HOW KAKA WON LAND OTTER POWER

THE
venerated Kaka was the first person to confront the dreaded land otter and gain its powerful spirit. But instead of going into the woods to seek the land otter, he won its spirit power by his forceful resistance to the will of the Land Otter People, who had captured him. He had refused to be

13

brainwashed by the kushtakas.

Kaka did not seek the experience that led to his eminent status. It was thrust upon him indirectly through the wiles of his dissatisfied wife. But the same traits that had helped him become the highest chief in his village, as implied by his name Kaka (Tlingit for "Man-at-the-Top"), contributed to the successful outcome of his adventure with the kushtakas.

Kaka's wife was to blame for his capture in the first place. A favorite daughter of the chief, she was used to being pampered. Though she knew before her marriage that the demands of her husband's office would require much of his time and energy, she thought she would be able to coax him away from them frequently. But she had not been successful and found herself alone much of the time. She missed his favors when major hunts required him to avoid her for long periods in order to be clean for the reception of the hunting spirits. During puberty training she had learned that men had to avoid the "polluting influence" of women before battles, raids, and hunts. But she had not realized how often this would be and how restless she would become. So Kaka's wife looked for amusement elsewhere.

She found it in a handsome young man, and after the usual secret trysts they fell in love. Then they began to plan a way to get rid of Kaka. The wife hit upon an idea that would also test her lover's mettle.

"Get me the tail of a land otter," she demanded.

He blanched at her request, which would daunt even the bravest. Not only was the task extremely difficult, but since land otters were believed to lure people to their dens and transform them into Land Otter People, nobody wanted anything to do with them. But embolded by love, the young man took on the task and in a few days returned with a land otter's tail.

His lover praised his bravery and prowess. "Now skin it," she ordered. Again he did as he was told and presented her with the sinewy cord that ran through the tail.

That night the wife used all her feminine charms on her husband, Kaka. She brushed her long black hair until it was shiny and let it hang down to her waist. She was all smiles when he came in to dinner, and she sat beside him, catering to his every whim. Kaka, usually preoccupied, noticed her attentiveness.

"You're in great spirits tonight," he said.

"It has been so long since we have been together," she murmured, rolling her large black eyes up to him and then casting them down modestly.

"Ah, you have missed me. We shall make it up tonight," he answered, pulling her to him with a hug. She snuggled up to him and pulled his head onto her shoulder, petting it as she did so. Then she brushed her hand across his ear, at the same time lacing the tail sinew through the slit in the lobe for ear ornaments. Of course had he felt it, he would have stopped her, for to wear anything associated with land otters would make a person vulnerable to their destructive power. But she continued to distract him with her loving attention, making Kaka a happy man.

Kaka went out fishing as usual the next day, and in the early morning calm was making good time when, as he approached the point, the water became extremely rough. An expert boatman, he would ordinarily have guided his canoe ahead with little effort. But he felt himself losing control, and all at once the canoe flipped over.

Meanwhile the Land Otter People who lived under

the point had been watching Kaka as he became disoriented under the influence of their spirit power and now rushed out in their canoe to "save" him. One of them, in the guise of his father's servant, stretched out a hand to him. But Kaka knew better than to accept such help. He clung to his capsized hull and fought off the kushtakas' offers for several days. It was only when he realized that he was lost at sea and had no chance of getting back to his family and friends that he agreed to go with them.

Once in their canoe, he must have become unconscious, for he suddenly found himself in their den under the point. At first he thought that he was home, since it looked very much like his own house in the village, and things here were being done in much the same way as at home. Only the food was different. What appeared to be a good meal was only codfish heads and bones, and soon Kaka's mouth was all cut and disfigured from trying to eat them.

When Kaka did not return by evening, his relatives became concerned. He was a skilled boatman and the weather had been fairly calm. What could have detained him? They waited two more days and then went to the spot where he usually fished. At first they found nothing, but later in the day they sighted his overturned canoe in the water.

"How could this have happened to Kaka?" asked one of the men. "I have seen him manage a canoe in the wildest storm." Of course, they knew nothing of the land otter sinew in his ear, which had the spirit power that could cause him to become distracted.

"He could not have swum to shore from here," another man remarked. "He must have drowned."

"Or the kushtakas have 'saved' him," said another.

"Kushtakas! Kaka is too strong-willed to be won over by kushtakas," the first man retorted. They went back to the village with their sad news.

Search parties looked for Kaka for several days, but when they found nothing, the family gave a potlatch for him, since he was the nephew of a rich man. Instead of putting the food into the fire, as they did in the case of ordinary deaths, they put it into the water for him. For they were afraid if he ate the Land Otters' food, he would never be able to return home again. During the potlatch Kaka's uncle Ixt, who was also the shaman, asked the spirits to protect his nephew and to help the searchers find him. Then the rescuers set out once again.

Kaka's absence lasted for two long years. During this time his friends, led by his uncle Ixt, continued to hunt for him, enduring long fasts and periods of keeping away from their wives. But when Ixt's spirit failed to find him the family gave up looking.

"He's lost in the woods or drowned," they said. Nobody dared mention what they really feared — that the Land Otter Men had captured him. Ixt's spirit continued to tell him that Kaka was alive, but the shaman, persuaded by his relatives' doubts, no longer believed him.

"Why does my spirit say Kaka is alive, when he can be found nowhere?" the shaman asked. "Has my spirit lost the power to aid me?" And he fell into despair. So the spirit's voice was stilled and Kaka was not found.

Although Kaka lived with the Land Otter People all this time, they were not able to gain control over his mind to turn him against his family. Every day he thought of his relatives and longed to return to his home in the village. It was the memory of home and family that kept his resolve **17** alive and prevented him from taking on the nature of the Land Otter People.

One afternoon when all the Land Otter Men went out to hunt sea lions, the old woman who always sat in the corner called to him. "Come here. I want to tell you something." Kaka obeyed. "You are my nephew. I was captured by the Land Otter Men years ago."

Kaka was amazed at this revelation. He could see little resemblance to the aunt who had disappeared. As he drew closer he noticed hair on her hands and arms and neck — everywhere except on her face. Her arms were foreshortened and grew out of her breast like otters' forepaws. Her face did look like his aunt's, but the upper lip was pulled up to the nose to resemble an otter's. Repulsed, he drew away, but she came after him.

"I will tell you how you got here," she said, as she reached up and drew the otter tail from his ear. "See this cord? It is from the tail of a land otter. Your wife laced it through the hole in your ear for ornaments, and that is what attracted the Land Otter People to you."

Kaka could not believe such a thing of his wife. He remembered her sweetness to him the night before he left.

"That can't be true," he cried. "She was so loving on our last night together."

"It was all an act," his aunt said. "She had a lover and they wanted you out of the way. My poor nephew, it is she who has caused you all this suffering."

At first Kaka was sad and hurt. He thought of his lovely wife and her long shiny black hair and large eyes with their hint of mischief. Then be became angry. She had been false to him, and his people probably knew about it. How foolish he felt, how humiliated.

"She shall suffer for this, believe me."

Freed from the land otter's sinew, he began to see things more clearly. This was not his home. No wonder the food was so bad. Otter food. Ugh! Would he ever be able to return home? Though he had kept his distance from all of the creatures, he eventually gave in to a young Land Otter Woman who was kind to him and taught him many of their ways — things to make his life with them more bearable. She had helped him in his loneliness and he had agreed to marry her. Would she be able to help him now? He hurried to her and begged for help to return to his own home.

"But there is nothing I can do," she said. "The men rule here." She was hoping to keep him in the Land Otters' realm, for she loved him dearly and did not want to lose him.

"I want to go back home!" Kaka cried out in rage. "You tell your people to take me home or I will kill all of them!" But even as he spoke, he saw that he could barely lift his arms. When he was finally able to raise them, he found he had no feeling in his body. Land otter spirit power was exerting its influence on him, for though he had resisted becoming a Land Otter Man, he was still physically subject to their power. His young wife took pity on Kaka and went to plead with her uncle the Land Otter chief to take him back to his home. Better to have her loved one happy at home than miserable here.

At first, the Land Otter chief refused.

"But Father, it's been two years now that we've been trying to control Kaka's mind. If we haven't done so now, we will never succeed."

The chief had to agree. "I will let him go," he said with reluctance, for Kaka would have been a fine acquisition. "I will take him back home, but I will give him the land otter spirit to use among his people so they will know how great its power is. This man has proved himself to be a worthy vehicle, for he has shown great mental discipline and strong will power. He will use this spirit power for healing the sick, foretelling the future, and finding those who are lost. He will be held in highest regard by his people."

Kaka's young wife was delighted that her husband had been chosen for such a great mission. "At least he will take part of us with him," she said.

The chief called his brothers-in-law to him to ask for their help, and four of them set out with him and Kaka in a canoe. As they came out into the water from under the rocky ledge, Kaka saw purple starfish clinging to the barnacled rocks under water and sea anemone and jelly fish inching their way around the canoe.

When the Land Otter Men forced him to lie in the bottom of the boat, Kaka noticed that it looked strange. He had heard that the Land Otter Men used a skate for the canoe and minks as their paddles. Were they riding a skate now? They covered him with a mat so he could not see what they were doing or where they were going.

When he did look up once, though, he saw that he was tangled among the kelp stems. Were they going under water, or was the kelp floating? He could not think clearly. He seemed to be in a daze, and a strange feeling came over him. He was being possessed by land otter power.

"These land otters are going to become my spirits," he realized.

He had also noticed that it was dark out.

"They must travel by night and sleep during the day," he thought. "But, of course, that fits; it is in the night that they hunt their food."

The second day that the Land Otter brothers-in-laws were rowing Kaka toward home, they overslept. It was late evening before they started rowing again and almost dawn as they drew near the shore. Afraid that Raven would crow before they reached land and thus bring about their death, the Land Otter Men scrambled for the beach. Now looking more like otters than men, they scattered to hide behind bushes and rocks. Kaka was left to pull up the canoe, which had, at Raven's call, decidedly taken the form of a skate. This spine back of the fish chafed the skin of his lower arms as he struggled to bring the "canoe" ashore.

Alone now with his land otter spirits, Kaka set out for the nearest town. He did not dare reveal himself to the people, sensing that he had undergone a great change. When he came to some fish and kelp drying in the sun, he just helped himself. People could see the food disappear but could not see anyone taking it, although they did hear rustling noises. When they took the food in and put it away in baskets, Kaka tried to make himself visible to ask for food. But that was not successful either. The people could see only his shadow, and the sight of it caused them to get sleepy.

"That's Kaka's shadow!" cried one of the fishermen as he caught a glimpse of it. "Let's get him and take him to the chief." They ran after the shadow, but whenever they got close to it, they began to feel drowsy.

Others who saw his shadow called out, "Kaka, you have already turned into a groundhog." They said this in hopes of keeping him from turning into a Land Otter Man, for they were fairly certain that he was trying to return from the Land Otter kingdom.

Though Kaka continued to elude them, they felt his presence. At night he would take fish that had been hung out on lines to dry. He was behaving like a kushtaka. A stakeout was set out by the line, and sure enough, when night came they could see it moving in the moonlight and the fish disappearing. Then they decided to set a snare to catch him; they spaced nails out of sight along the lines. At first the nails only cut Kaka's hands, but after a while, contact with the metal began to bring back Kaka's human form. For besides warding off land otter power, metal could also take away its effect. Shadows would then take their human forms, and onlookers would not lose consciousness in the presence of land otter spirit power.

When Kaka's body became firm enough for the people to hold, they seized him and took him home on a stretcher. They noticed that his body was covered lightly all over with fur except for his face. His hands and feet were more thickly furred. He had bruises everywhere from crawling on the sharp rocks without shoes or clothing.

On Kaka's arrival, his shaman uncle Ixt called on his animal spirit to help bring Kaka to his full senses. As Kaka became partially conscious, his mother's family tried to feed him, but he pushed them away. They brought a tray of tasty fish when he was fully conscious, but he brushed that aside too, upsetting it and scattering the fish all around. Then he hid his face in his hand and sat by the fire.

As time went by he began to take bits of food and to regain his strength. Then he remembered what his Land Otter aunt had told him, and he felt the anger and humiliation returning.

"My wife betrayed me," he told his uncle. "It was she who made me easy prey for the Land Otter People by lacing a sinew from a land otter tail through the hole in my ear for ornaments." Ixt gasped, but Kaka went on. "I resisted going with them at first, but I finally had to give in or die. They were never able to control my mind completely. I think that is why they agreed to bring me back."

Ixt was shocked to hear of the wife's treachery and angered by it.

"Take the wily woman out at low tide and tie her to a rock below the tideline," he ordered the men. "Leave her there to drown as the tide comes in."

The people gathered in silence to watch the woman being led down to the reef. Kaka's heart ached as he watched her walk, pale and straight-backed, to the place of her death. She had been so dear to him. Should he call them back? Even if he wanted to, he could not. The chief's order must be followed. Treachery must be punished. The sight filled all who watched with horror, but the people felt the punishment was proper.

Only after justice had been done did Kaka regain his appetite and eventually his full strength. He told the people about the kushtakas — what they looked like, how they behaved, what their homes were like. The spirits he had gained in his struggle against the land otter power stayed with him and made him a most powerful shaman — the first one ever to return from the world of the Land Otter People in possession of their spirit power.

THE CHALLENGE

IT was the height of salmon season, and four boys in their early teens were idling along the beach. They were not quite old enough to man the large fishing boats that went out for as long as fourteen hours in the busy season. Their job was to help unload when the boats returned laden with fish. But that would be some time, for they had just left. Now, as they watched the fish jumping in the bay, the boys were eager to do some fishing of their own.

"Let's paddle over to Humpy Creek. I bet it's full of salmon," said the nephew of the chief. The youngest of the four, he was being groomed as the chief's successor. His three older companions were supposed to stay with him and keep him from danger.

On their way to get permission to leave, the four boys saw the shaman Ducksta talking to the women and those men too old to go fishing. In no mood on such a sunny morning to listen to one of his lectures, the boys changed direction slightly to avoid him.

"Times have been good for us in recent years," Ducksta was reminding his small audience. "Fish and game are plentiful, and no other clans have threatened us. In some ways this is good. But it has dampened the spirit of the young men. They see no reason to compete to become great warriors and hunters."

"They do not take the rituals seriously," one of the men interrupted. "Last week I saw the oldest companion of the chief's nephew throw the bones of a salmon on the beach instead of returning them to the stream."

"Their uncles are not strict enough with the boys," another added. "They have become careless themselves."

Ducksta had seen the boys going down to the beach and knew they had avoided him. He would have done the same in those carefree days of his youth, before he accepted the shaman spirit. He remembered his own resistance to inheriting the spirit power of his dead uncle, the previous shaman. Unready to take on that responsibility, he had become extremely ill. When the medicine men were brought in to work over him, they told him he had been "called" and that his resistance to this gift was causing his severe illness. He had no choice but to accept the spirit power and learn to control it. Life became a more serious matter once he had assumed that great responsibility.

"When the men come back from fishing tonight, I will talk to them," Ducksta said. "We must insist on careful practice of tribal rituals."

The boys caught only snatches of the conversation as they continued to push their boat out. It was a beautiful day to be on the water, warm with a gentle breeze. To reach the creek, they had to go out into the open water for several miles to a cove on the other side of the island. Muscular and fit, the boys paddled easily in smooth, rhythmic motions and soon reached the mouth of the creek, where they pulled the boat onto the rocks and tied it to a log. Then they grabbed their lines and started to fish, there at the mouth of the stream where salmon were swarming, and soon had a huge catch.

"Let's start a fire and cook fish," the chief's nephew said. "I'm starved."

They built a fire from driftwood and put rocks in it to heat. Then one boy dug a pit in the sand while the others looked for skunk cabbage leaves. They lined the pit with the heated rocks, covered them with the leaves, and then placed the salmon, also wrapped in cabbage leaves, on the rocks to bake. But the fish were a long time baking and the boys grew restless. They needed more action.

"Let's build a bigger fire and cook more fish," said the oldest. They scrambled for more wood and rocks and built a fire higher up on the bank. Then they went back to their fishing.

27

The fish came even faster than before. One after the other the boys pulled salmon out of the water, and with each fish their excitement grew. Soon they had another large stack of salmon. Their exhilaration grew near to frenzy. Grabbing as many fish as they could hold in their arms, they ran up the bank to the new fire. But now, totally out of control, they lost all sense of proper behavior. Instead of digging a pit in the sand, the oldest boy began throwing his fish directly onto the hot rocks in the fire. One salmon was still alive.

"Look at that one squiggle on the rocks!" he yelled. "Listen to it sizzle!" They all laughed, and others threw their fish on the hot rocks, too, jumping with joy at the snapping and popping sounds.

Again, it was the oldest boy who grabbed a frog making its way up the bank and flung it into the fire. While the creature frantically hopped around trying to escape, the boys jumped and laughed as it wriggled in pain.

But a feeling of uneasiness soon came over the chief's nephew, and he began to recall his grandmother's teachings. "All animals should be treated with respect," she had so often told him, "especially the frog, which has special meaning for our clan." How had he let himself forget? He realized then that in their excitement, he and his friends had broken basic clan rules. He began to fear repercussions. Sobered, he called to his companions.

"I think the fish in the pit are ready now. Let's eat." The other boys may also have been having second thoughts, for they became unduly quiet as they settled down to eat. After dinner they cleaned the rest of the fish and put them into the boat with the earlier catch. Then they pushed the loaded canoe into the water and set off for home.

The return trip went more slowly, for the load was heavy, and the boys were tired from the day's activities. The first hour or so was uneventful, but when they had gone about half way, a sudden wind came up and the water became very choppy. Huge whitecaps and deep waves flung the small boat about. For all their skill in handling canoes, the boys were hard put to keep the boat from overturning. They paddled desperately.

"Look!" cried the nephew. "The boat's filling up!"

"Paddle harder!" the oldest called. "We need more power to keep the boat on top of the waves."

"There goes my paddle," cried one of the boys, as a rush of water swept it out of his hands. The small craft rose on the crest of each wave and then dropped hard into the trough.

Soon they had all lost their paddles, and it was all they could do to hold onto the sides of the canoe. Suddenly the overloaded canoe swamped and capsized, throwing the boys into the sea. Though all were good swimmers, they had trouble finding the boat in the dark.

"Here it is!" the oldest shouted, and the others struggled to grab hold. They called loudly for help, but no one else was out at that hour. The cold water numbed their hands as they tried to hold on. They had stopped kicking to save strength and were resting against the side of the overturned hull. Their grips were beginning to loosen. If help did not come soon, they would drown.

Then, through the dark haze, they saw what looked like the outline of a canoe coming toward them.

"Who are those people?" asked the nephew, straining to see better.

"It looks like some of our relatives," the oldest **29**

answered as the boat drew nearer.

"Hey, I guess we were closer to home than we thought," said another, as all the boys began to recognize uncles and cousins. Their arrival gave the boys a spurt of energy.

"We have come to save you. Let us help you into our canoe," said the leader, stretching out his hand. The exhausted boys were all too ready to accept. Only the chief's nephew held back. Something his grandmother had said about people who suddenly appeared to rescue storm victims was tugging at his memory.

One by one the boys took the hand of the leader and were pulled into his canoe. At last, the chief's nephew reluctantly followed them. Better that than drown. The boys lay back in the boat, too dazed by cold and exhaustion to notice that it was not headed for the village or to remember that these rescuers, whom they recognized as relatives, had actually died at sea some time ago. They had heard that drowning victims were "saved" by Land Otter People, or kushtakas, and transformed into one of them. Then, lonely for their relatives, these saved people would lure them to the same fate. The chief's nephew remembered being drilled to refuse that kind of help.

"Resist firmly," his grandmother had told him. "A strong will can overcome even the Land Otter People. Sit daily in the icy water and chew devil's club to make your will strong as well as your body."

Now the chief's nephew realized that this advice was what had been pricking at his thoughts earlier. "I forgot about discipline today," he thought as he recalled joining in the wildness of the older boys and laughing with them at the tortures of the salmon and the frog. Now he was regretting those actions. Nearly inert from the cold, he had been unable to remember previous warnings and had not even considered that the rescuers might be Land Otter People.

But that is what they were. They were being led by One-Who-Was-Saved-by-the-Land-Otters, a man who had been "captured" at sea and transformed into a kushtaka, and who was now taking the boys to the Land Otters' den.

In the meantime, the boys' relatives were waiting back in the village for their return. At first they thought the boys might be waiting out the storm in a cove. But after the storm subsided and several days passed, they became alarmed.

"We must go search for the boys and see that they have not come to harm," the chief said. So the older brothers of the chief's nephew formed a rescue party and set out for Humpy Creek, where they found only the dead campfires.

"Where shall we look?" asked the leader. "Their boat is not here."

"Maybe they went to another village," suggested one brother.

"Or maybe they have been lost at sea," said the youngest, voicing what the others had been avoiding. They stood silent as they faced this possibility.

"Let's go consult the shaman Ducksta," the leader finally suggested. "He may be able to tell us what happened to the boys and how we can find them."

The men knew that the shaman possessed all kinds of powers. He could control the weather, foretell the future, cure the sick, and bring success in war or in hunting. But most important at this time, he could find those lost or captured by the Land Otter People and sometimes restore

31

them to their families and their normal human lives.

As soon as the returning searchers landed below the village, the men reported to the chief, who led them to the shaman's house. Ducksta stood before them dressed in ragged clothes that had been soaked in seal oil, his disheveled hair tied in a knot behind his head. Since a shaman's power was believed to reside in his hair, it was never combed or cut and often grew almost to his heels. Ducksta listened with care to their story.

"I must meditate and summon my spirits before deciding which powers to call upon for this job," he told them.

"We understand that, Honored Shaman, and are prepared to reward your efforts with blankets sewn by the women of our clan," said the chief, displaying the gifts he had brought. Ducksta was pleased with the offering.

"Call the people together to witness the summons of the spirits," the shaman answered. "Clear the hall of guns and women, as they keep the spirits away." The shaman himself would have to stay away from weapons and women as well as fast for several days before contacting the spirits.

On the appointed day, Ducksta took his place in the center of the hall. He removed his clothes and loosened his floor-length hair, letting it drape around his body. Then he sat on a large carved box with his back to the fire. For a long time he sat in silence while he tried to communicate with his spirits.

Ducksta was an old shaman, highly respected by his people. He had visited the woods often in his youth and gained the spirit powers of many different animals. But the land otter spirit was his strongest. It is the first animal spirit a shaman seeks out, but a wise shaman goes back often to the woods to strengthen that power. Now Ducksta remained motionless for hours, waiting for the spirit to speak to him. Suddenly he moved slightly and faint gurgled sounds came from his mouth. His attendant had to interpret them for the people.

"The great Ducksta has called on Kluqua, his land otter spirit, and repeated to him your generous offer of blankets. Kluqua will accept the mission." The people murmured approval. The attendant went on.

"Four of our young braves have disappeared, the shaman has told Kluqua. They left here several days ago to fish at Humpy Creek, but the rescue party found only two dead campfires on the bank. Ducksta has ordered Kluqua to go to the camp and see what he can discover." Joyful sounds came from the people.

In the manner of spirits, Kluqua left for the camp and came back within minutes.

"I, too, found only two dead campfires," he told the shaman. "But among the ashes was a dead frog that had burned."

Ducksta groaned. He knew the frog would not have jumped into the fire on its own accord. One of the boys must have thrown it there. And he knew the terrible punishment that such disrespect could bring, not only to the boys but to the whole clan. The people, who could not see Kluqua, heard only the groans and did not know what to make of Ducksta's pained movements.

"Go look for the boys on the water," the assistant said, interpreting Ducksta's command to Kluqua. The spirit power was off again. This time his errand took longer.

Ducksta continued to moan and make utterances that only the assistant understood. "He fears we have lost the **33** young prince and there will be more trouble to come," he interpreted. Then Kluqua was before the shaman again.

"I found their capsized canoe floating on the water," he reported. "Right away I suspected they had been captured by the Land Otter People. So I checked their camp and saw the boys there." The people gasped at the attendant's report. Then they became angry.

"We must get them back!" the oldest boy's uncle shouted.

As other relatives joined in the angry threats, the chief quieted them, saying, "We must hold a meeting of the council to decide what action to take."

At the council meeting the men decided to smoke the Land Otter People away from their dens by burning spruce gum at the openings. They went out to gather masses of spruce gum, loading it into canoes to take to the mouths of the dens. The seriousness of their actions, almost a challenge to the dreaded Land Otter People, made them somber.

Toward evening they set out in the loaded canoes for the place indicated by Ducksta and arrived at dark. They pulled the boats up onto the beach with care, hoping to take the sleeping kushtakas by surprise. Quietly they unloaded the spruce gum and put it in piles near the den openings. Then they set it afire, and when it blazed high, poured urine on it to make a strong smoke that would asphyxiate those inside and also ward off any evil spirits that the Land Otter People might use in their counterattack. Then they ran back to their canoes and waited to see what happened. In the dark, acrid smoke billowing up from the fires, they could see shadowy forms of some kushtakas or land otters rushing about, trying to escape the suffocating fumes.

34

When the fires died down after many hours, four men were chosen to scout the dens. As they stole up the beach, listening for signs of life, the others waited tensely and watched them disappear into the openings. After a long time the scouts returned.

"Everyone who is in the caves is dead," they reported, "including the four boys."

Their word sent up a wail among the people, devastated to know what they had done, for they had meant only to smoke out the Land Otters and demand the return of the boys. But now the boys were dead. The grieving relatives took only slight consolation from knowing that many kushtakas had been killed too, for that meant certain retaliation. They returned in sorrow to their village.

As they passed the pond by the lake, one of the rescuers remembered something. "Two land otters escaped into this pond while the fire was still burning," he said.

"One was white and the other was dark," another added. Others remembered seeing them too. The men went in silence to the boats.

Several days later, some of the men returning from a seal hunt were rounding the cape close to their village when they saw what appeared to be two black loons and a gull sitting on the rocks. But as they reached shore they saw there were really two black land otters bringing fish to a white one.

"That's the white otter that escaped from the fire," shouted the man who had seen it diving into the pond. The hunters paddled quickly to shore, jumped from the boat, and surrounded the animal. As they tried to pick it up, it squirmed and slithered out of their arms. One man hurried back to the boat for a cedar-bark mat, which they finally managed to wrap around the white otter. As they carried it toward home, one black otter, One-Who-Was-Saved, who had come to the dead boys' "rescue," flapped quietly behind the men, staying at a discreet distance and taking in their conversation.

Finding the white otter reminded the men that they had still not atoned for massacring many Land Otter People.

"Why don't we give the Land Otter People a potlatch?" suggested one of the men. It was customary to invite members of a hostile tribe to a potlatch as a peace measure, and they discussed possibilities as they went.

When they reached the village, they called the people to see the beautiful white land otter they had captured. Others who had taken part in the smoke-out also recognized it as the one that had escaped. While the villagers were standing around admiring the white otter, the men suggested having a potlatch to appease the Land Otter People.

"The white land otter can be the Peacemaker," someone suggested. The crowd agreed and carried the white otter into the house, setting it on a new cedar mat in the place of honor across the room from the door. As they did this they noticed a change come over the otter. It took on a furry human face and form, the form of a kushtaka.

They set about painting this Land Otter Man's face for the Peacemaker role. They painted the mouth red and the eyebrows green. On the cheeks they made two round red spots and around them drew two blue lines to represent the bow and stern of a canoe coming to make peace. From the left side of the forehead to the right cheek they painted a narrow green diagonal line to represent the pole that pushes the canoe along. Then, as a sign of peace and friendship, they scattered eagle-down on and around the Land Otter Man. They kept fires burning all night to keep their honored guest comfortable.

In the meantime One-Who-Was-Saved, who had continued behind the fishermen and taken in the whole discussion, dashed back to the Land Otter People's camp. He hurried into each of the dens, inviting everyone to the potlatch and telling them of the villagers' plans to make peace.

Ordinarily the potlatch guests received a formal invitation from a delegate of the hosts. When the guests were ready to visit the village, the delegate would lead them to the shore of the host village and go up to announce their arrival. The host group would then come to welcome them with a peace song and dance. But in this case, the hosts had no idea the guests had been invited.

As morning began to dawn, the villagers awoke to find a heavy fog rolling in around the cape. They seemed to hear singing and drums in the direction of the fog, but they could see no one. As the fog drifted in, they could hear the songs more plainly but did not recognize the voices.

"Who is that singing? Who could be coming?" one of them asked. "Could it be our guests?"

"How would they know of the potlatch?" asked another. "We haven't sent the invitation yet. Let's wait inside until we can see who it is." Usually the potlatch visitors camped near the village until the host went out to welcome them with songs and dances. But these newcomers seemed to be taking things into their own hands. The people began to fear that these were not ordinary visitors on an ordinary mission. But a numbness was overcoming them, dulling their fear.

As the fog continued to roll in, the people in the hall began to feel drowsy and drifted off to sleep. Finally only Ducksta was awake to witness the coming of the Land Otter People.

The visitors went up to the community house where the white Peacemaker sat in the place of honor. One-Who-Was-Saved led the group, singing a song. He wore a land otter design on his headpiece, one painted on each shoulder, and one on his chest. In each hand he carried a rattle of puffin beaks. As he led the rhythm with his rattles, the Land Otter Women lined up and danced. It was only after the visitors had sung two songs and were drawing close to the third that the villagers began to come out of their trances. During the final song the Land Otter People picked up the Peacemaker and carried him out of the hall, disappearing as the song faded. The people, now fully awake, emerged from the hall and saw only a haze over the water and a rim of foam where the guests had been.

"Our guests did not wait for us to sing and dance for them," the leader remarked to the shaman.

"It was the Land Otter People," Ducksta groaned, "and they have not accepted our offer of peace. Now we must wait to see what they will do."

"Let us stay for a few days until we find out what they're up to," said the chief, knowing that the Land Otter People's retaliation could be vicious.

For some time the people stayed close to their homes, fishing and hunting nearby. But after a while some of the younger ones grew restless.

"Let's go over to Warm Chuck Lake," suggested one of the livelier boys. "I know where a canoe is cached."

His three friends were game, but they had to get

permission from the older men first.

"You can't go out," an older man warned. "The Land Otter People are angry."

"Maybe the Land Otter People meant only to get the white otter back," another suggested. "Maybe they don't intend to retaliate further."

"Let them go," a third said. "Boys can't be cooped up for long." So the boys were allowed to go. They found the canoe hidden in the brush, put it into the water, and started to paddle toward the head of the lake. As they approached the north shore, they were startled by a figure that looked like a frog but was dressed in a bearskin. In a strident voice he called to the boys and motioned them toward him. Terrified but not daring to disobey, the boys paddled closer to the strange being. Then he began to speak.

"I have a message for Ducksta, your shaman," his voice boomed out. "Return to your village and tell him to hurry here to see a shaman stronger than himself, for death will come to him soon."

The boys nodded, too frightened to answer. They knew that shamans from hostile villages challenged each other's spirit powers, the one with the most spirits overcoming the opponent. The boys also were familiar with the ordeal shamans went through to gain an animal's spirit power. First the shaman-to-be went into the woods to fast for eight days. Then he waited for the animal to come. When it did, he waved a picklike club before it, and if his preparation had been right, the creature dropped dead at his feet. Then he cut out the animal's tongue or sliced a piece from it, bound it tightly with roots of devil's club, and hid it in a dry place for future use. The spirit power stayed in the tongue and entered into the shaman.

"This shaman must have gone often into the woods for the spirit powers of many animals," the older boy said, "or he would not dare to challenge the great Ducksta."

Though the land otter was the first spirit to come to a shaman, most shamans went on other retreats into the woods to gain new spirits or to strengthen a power they already possessed. But no shaman was known to have gained more than eight animal spirits.

"And there is more," the shaman's booming voice called. "For the disrespect of your people to the salmon and the frog, you shall die." The boys gasped. They had done nothing to the frog or salmon, but the lost boys evidently had, and they now understood that the clan was being held responsible.

"To show you my great power, I utter this omen," the shaman went on. "As soon as you start for home, the first of you shall drop dead. In the center of the lake, the second shall die. When you reach the lake's outlet, the third shall die. Only the fourth shall live until he gives my message to Ducksta. Then he too shall fall dead."

Shaking with fright, the boys ran for the boat and pushed off from shore. Nobody spoke. Would the shaman's prediction come true? Who would be the first to die? Just a few yards from shore, a boy in the middle of the boat fell over, dead. The others looked on in horror but kept rowing as fast as they could. Would another die at the center of the lake? Who would it be?

As they neared the center, a second boy fell over. For the rest of the trip the other two eyed each other with alarm, wondering who would be spared to take the message to Ducksta. As they came to the creek that was the lake's outlet, the third boy died. Now only the leader was left, the

40

one who had found the cached canoe and suggested the trip. He grieved at the loss of his friends and dreaded having to die so soon himself. It took all of his resolve to paddle his leaden load back down the creek to the village.

When he drew up to the beach, the villagers were stunned at the sight of three boys dead in the canoe. The survivor was too numb to answer their questions. He went directly to Ducksta's home and as briefly as possible told of the canoe trip and the deaths of the boys by the shaman's curse. Then he braced himself for the final message.

"The mighty shaman has ordered you to go visit him, that you might see a shaman stronger than yourself," he said to Ducksta. "He says that you are soon to die." Then, as the challenging shaman had predicted, the boy fell dead. The people drew back in terror. Ducksta cried out in grief and anger at the boys' deaths brought on by the shaman's curse.

"Who is this that visits death upon our innocent youth and issues an insulting challenge to my power?" he shouted. He could sense the people's fear and feel their confidence in him shrinking.

"Do not be afraid, my people. I shall confront this braggart and bring him to his knees." Then as the people took the bodies into the house to prepare them for burial, Ducksta went off by himself to get ready to meet his challenger.

"I must go into the woods to renew my spirit powers," Ducksta said to his assistant. "It has been many years since I have done so. I renewed them often when I was younger, but I have become careless in recent years. Now with this threat from a powerful shaman I shall need all the power I can muster."

He told his assistant to prepare for the trip, and **41**

together they went deep into the woods. The muskeg was soft underfoot, and red and green moss lined their path. Stunted cedar bushes growing among the spruce trees mingled with the wildflowers and small labrador tea plants to give off a sweet scent. There were bear signs and spiked holes from deer hooves and a pond that beavers had made by damming the stream to weaken the tree trunks, making them easier to cut down. But this scene of untouched beauty did little to lift Ducksta's heavy spirits. His thoughts were still on the tragic events involving the village.

"We have been too lax in training the young people, especially the nephew of the chief who was to succeed him. With stricter discipline the boys would have shown respect for the frog and salmon," he mused aloud, but even as he said this, he understood the boys' high spirits. It took spirit to be a leader — a disciplined spirit. The young prince had not exercised control.

The walk into the woods brought back the memory of his first fast to acquire his spirit powers. As soon as he was strong enough, he had chosen an assistant and gone into the woods for his first fast and preparation. Shortly after the prescribed eight days were up, he had experienced the trance. By then, his skin had become almost transparent from lack of food or drink, and his eyes were glassy. As he felt the approach of the spirits, Ducksta had begun to dance and was soon whirling in a frenzy. Then he had fallen to the ground. The trees swayed overhead, their branches whipping and undulating above him. They seemed to be closing in on him. He lost consciousness for a while and then had wakened to find his assistant bending over him, trying to revive him. He stayed in a semiconscious trance, icy cold, yet able to feel things crawling over his body and face, the way insects would feel. Then he seemed to be floating in an eddying pool, his heart pounding in his chest. Lining the edges of the pool were land otters, all staring hard at him. Suddenly he had felt a surge of power within himself, as though he could accomplish anything. The otter spirit powers were coming to him, and he could feel and hear their urgings. But when he tried to repeat their messages, his words came out as gurglings that only his assistant, who had fasted with him, could understand. Once the boy had become totally conscious, he and his assistant had gone to find a land otter and cut its tongue.

But that was many years ago. Now on this return to the woods, Ducksta could feel some of the old stirrings. He entered into the fast with the determination of his youth, but without the vigor of youth, the eight-day ordeal was much harder. His hands shook from hunger and his bones ached from cold. Too much time had passed since his last trip into the woods to renew his spirit powers. He felt no strong spirit power raging wihin him and no urge to do a frenzied dance. But a feeling of peace and courage warmed him from within, and he began to sense what he must do. Just as in his youth, when he had accepted the call to the shaman's life, he now accepted the role thrust upon him, regardless of the consequences. He would go back to his village, don his full shaman regalia, and go to meet the challenge.

As the people came to meet him on his return home, he could see fear in their faces.

"Take courage, my people," he said. "I have spoken to my spirits and I shall don my regalia and go in honor to face the challenger." He left them comforted as he motioned his assistant to go with him.

First he put on the skin apron, painted with two killer whales face-to-face across the middle, and fringed along the bottom with puffin beaks. Around his waist he wrapped a belt of braided cedar bark and then tied his wooden greaves on his legs. Next he put on his necklace and bracelets of ivory and bone amulets and laced the bone charm through the septum of his nose. The assistant blackened Ducksta's face with charcoal. Then upon his head he set the headdress of ermine that cascaded down his back, and over it the goat-horn crown. Finally Ducksta gathered his beaded blanket around him and went outside to speak to the people.

The people looked at him in awe. It had been a long time since they had seen him in full regalia.

"How stately he looks," said one. "He moves with such sure strides."

"Look how fierce his face is. Surely he will terrify the intruder."

"See the glow about him," a third man said. "Surely spirit powers are with him." And the people began to take heart.

Then Ducksta spoke to them.

"I have served you well for many years with courage and shrewdness. My last mission was to find the boys taken by the Land Otter People. This I did, but it has brought us much sorrow. Now I must meet their shaman. If I should be defeated, give me a proper burial and think well of me in death."

Then he walked to the center of the village, faced the mountains, and bellowed in his loudest voice.

"My spirit power is from above and below. Nothing can harm me, not even the mighty Land Otter shaman's power." As his voice resounded through the village, the people were filled with pride and courage and gathered round him. They too would stand up to the Land Otter People.

But no sooner did his voice reach the dwelling of the Land Otter shaman, than Ducksta began to bleed at the mouth. Before the echo of his mighty challenge had died, he fell to the ground. The people cried out as his assistant rushed to him. But the great Ducksta was dead.

Then the people heard a loud voice echo through the village: "I am Kushtaka, the mighty Land Otter Man. In my time I have cut four land otter tongues, and their spirit power has entered into me. I also have the spirit power of four other animals. My strength is greater than that of any living shaman!"

At first the people were filled with fear. What would happen to them now? Their shaman was dead and the Land Otter People were sure to attack them. But their fear soon turned to anger. Who was this great shaman that he should cause the death of their beloved Ducksta?

"He is the Land Otter shaman," answered the chief. "He has taken the life of Ducksta in retaliation for the death of the Land Otter People we smoked out of the dens with the spruce gum fire. Now we must get ready to meet the Land Otter People, who will soon attack us."

He led the men in to prepare their weapons for battle. Though their hearts were heavy at the thought of almost certain defeat, they were determined to fight fiercely before going to their deaths. Ducksta's gallant stand had given them heart.

But while they were making their preparations, the mighty Kushtaka spoke again.

"The death of the great Ducksta has given satisfaction **45** for the death of our people at your hands," he said. "We will seek no further vengeance."

With great relief, the people put away their war weapons and got ready to give Ducksta a proper burial. Next they would have to find out who among them had the spirit powers worthy to be his successor. They vowed to honor their tribal traditions more closely in the future and to train the young people also to hold him in the highest regard — and to be wary of the kushtakas at all times.

LAND OTTER SISTER

IT was springtime, and the village larders were all empty, so the men set out earlier than usual in the season to try to find fish. One man went with his wife and children to a certain point to catch halibut. The weather was still cold, and the skin capes they wore to keep dry whipped in the wind. There was little to eat yet, only a few shellfish and whatever they were able to pick from the beach at low tide. Fish would be plentiful in the summer, but not now.

The first thing the man did was to build a house from wide sheets of bark he had skinned from trees over the winter and had brought with him. He cut alder to make poles and crosspieces for an A-shaped frame, over which he spread the bark. Nearby he built a shed from hemlock branches to cover a frame for drying fish. In the meantime the man's wife and children dug clams and gathered cockles and other shellfish on the beach. They used their food sparingly, setting some aside for the coming days, for it would take quite a while for the husband to build a canoe to go out for halibut.

Once the houses were finished, the husband went into the woods to look for a tall straight cedar with no lower branches to spoil the even grain. When he found the tree he thought would do, he stripped bark from a ring around the base, and with his ax began to chop at the bared wood. With swift strong strokes he brought the tree down. Then he peeled the bark from the rest of the log, and with adze and hammer he split off a section along the side of the log that was to form the inside of the canoe. This side he laid downward so that he could begin to shape the canoe bottom.

First, working quickly with an ax, the man cut away the excess at each end and then began to shape it more deliberately with the adze. When he was satisfied with the outside shape of the hull, he turned the log over, flat side up once more, and hollowed it out slightly, fluffing up the oily chips to dry out a little. Then he started a fire with them, adding small sticks of wood when needed to keep it going. When the fire had burned a few days, the log became

48

charred enough to ease the process of hollowing it. When he had it hollowed to the desired thickness, he piled in rocks that had been heated in a fire and poured water over them to create steam. As the wood began to soften, he wedged a cross-brace into the midsection to force out the hull into a molded curve. After weeks of hard work, his small craft was ready to take him out to fish for halibut.

All the while the man and his family were working at their tasks, they were being watched from around the point by the husband's sister, who had become a kushtaka, or Land Otter Woman. After seemingly having drowned many years before, she had been captured by the Land Otter People and had become one of them.

To confront the Land Otter People was life's ultimate test. "Resist the kushtakas at all cost," grandmothers admonished children, and it remained a guiding principle throughout their lives. Children were also warned of wandering too far into the woods or water, the territory of the kushtakas. The spiritual and physical strength needed to resist was gained through diligent adherence to tribal ritual and code, such as bathing daily in the cold water and showing proper respect to animals.

The man's sister by now had married a Land Otter Man, and they had many children, who were busily gathering great quantities of food on the other side of the point. When she went back and told her husband that her brother and his family were nearby and in great need, he suggested that she help them.

"Take them some food from our larders," he said. "We have plenty of halibut, seal, salmon, and shellfish." The sister was delighted that he would let her help her relatives and set about packing a large basket to take them.

The night the basic hull was hollowed, the husband fell into bed, exhausted, and was deep in sleep when he was aroused by something outside the shelter. It sounded as though somebody had dropped a heavy pack there. Then he heard a voice.

"The place you are staying is wonderfully far from us."

"A place 'wonderfully far?'" the husband wondered. "Far from what?" He went out to investigate. There he saw a strange creature. It appeared to be a woman without shoulders, but with her arms growing out from her breast. There was a light film of hair on her face and her mouth was round, with the upper lip drawn up under her nose. When she turned to pick up the basket, he could see hair growing all over her back down to her seat. The creature noticed his astonished look and hurried to reassure him.

"It is I, your sister who drowned many years ago. I was captured at sea by the Land Otter People and married one of them. My husband and I live with our children around the point a short distance away."

"A short distance," thought the husband. "That must be what she meant by a place 'wonderfully far' — a pleasant walk from here."

Still dazed, he helped her carry the basket into the house, staying a safe distance behind her. "I wonder if this really is my sister or someone pretending to be her," he mused, staring at his visitor. "I wonder what this person is up to."

"Hurry and take the things out of the basket," he heard her urging him. "I have to get back home before Raven calls." The man unloaded the provisions as fast as he could, for he, too, believed that death would come to any living thing outside its home when the raven called at dawn.

Working as quietly as possible so as not to wake his sleeping wife and children, he had soon emptied the basket. As he looked up from setting down the last items, the basket and woman were nowhere to be found. Weary and amazed, he went back to bed and fell asleep.

When he awoke the next morning, he felt sure that his guest's appearance had been a dream. But then he saw all the provisions where he had put them.

"Where did all this food come from?" his wife asked. He told her as much as he could recall of the strange happening of the previous night, but he was a little hazy about details. Encounters with kushtakas often left people vague and uncertain. The wife gave each child a piece of dried fish and prepared some of the fresh fish for their dinner. The rest she put on the frame to dry to take back with her to the village.

Next evening the man's sister came again with a full basket. This time she appeared to his wife also. Although the husband had described the changes in his sister, the wife was shocked when she saw them for herself. She drew back in fear from her sister-in-law.

"Don't be afraid. I am your husband's sister and have come to help you," the visitor said in a kindly manner. Although still apprehensive, the wife invited her guest into the house.

"I have several children," the sister told the couple during her brief visit. "My three boys are older than yours. I'll bring them over tomorrow to help you get halibut and other fish." The idea of being able to catch halibut appealed to the man and wife and overcame their fears somewhat.

So the little otter-children came to visit their human uncle. Again he and his wife were at first shocked at what **51** they saw. There stood these three little nephews, human beings from the waist up, but below the waist, land otters with tails. The sister, who had come with the boys, sat down and quickly made herself at home. The couple's children stared at her and approached slowly as she called to them.

"Come here, little ones. I am your auntie who was lost at sea. These are your cousins." The children turned similar stares toward their young half-otter relatives. "Come, sit on my lap," she said lifting them up on her knees. Soon she began to sing to them: "Little tail, little tail growing down."

As she sang, tails began to grow down from the ends of their spines. Then the father saw what was happening. "What are you doing to my children?" he shrieked. "Stop that!"

His sister quickly slapped their bottoms. "Up goes the little tail! Up into the bottom," she sang as she patted each one, and the tails retracted and vanished. "Tails can be very helpful," she said to her brother.

But he shuddered at the suggestion. "The Land Otter Woman might be helpful," he thought, "but she isn't above trying to win recruits to the Land Otter kingdom." Later the woman departed, leaving her otter-children with their uncle, and hurried home before the raven's call.

The two boys were starry-eyed as they watched their otter-cousins propel themselves rapidly with their tails across the beach and then through the water. "Could we do that if we had tails, Mama?" they asked.

"Don't ask silly questions," she replied, alarmed. "Ordinary children don't have tails." She made sure to keep them in her sight all the while they played with their otter-cousins. The father also kept alert for anything the otter-children might do to bring his own children under kushtaka influence.

One evening, after the otter-nephews had been with him for some time, the man was putting finishing touches on his canoe.

"I wonder how I can get the canoe down to the water?" he was thinking to himself. Aware of his thoughts, the otter-nephews waited until everyone was asleep and then went out to the boat. Putting their tails under it, they pulled it down to the water, a phenomenal feat for such small creatures.

"How did the canoe get down into the water?" the man mused when he went outside the next morning. But by this time he had stopped wondering at all the strange happenings in his life. At least they were in his favor.

"I wish I had some devilfish for halibut bait," he thought as plans for his fishing trip went through his head. That evening after everyone was asleep, the nephews again went out. The next morning the man found several devilfish in front of his house.

"Where did these come from?" But he lost no time in cutting them up for bait.

When the otter-nephews went out with their uncle to fish, his own children were left at home. Halibut fishing was no activity for two restless little boys. The otter-nephews directed their uncle to a deep place in the channel where they knew halibut usually fed, and the man fixed his halibut hooks on his line. The V-shaped hooks were made from two pieces of wood bound together at the point of the V. The shorter piece had an ivory or bone spike that served as a hook to catch in the fish's mouth. A stone weight attached to a string hung from this shorter piece, causing it to float beneath the longer upper piece, on which was carved one of

53

the clan crest animals. The opening of the V was just large enough for the jaws of a medium-sized halibut. The jaws of smaller ones could not close on it, and halibut too big for the canoe could not get their jaws into the opening.

After fixing a piece of devilfish on the spike of each hook, the man dropped the lines into the water. Immediately the little otter-nephews went over the side and lowered themselves down the line. They watched for good-sized halibut to swim by and then quickly hooked them on the spikes. By keeping busy at this activity most of the afternoon, they were able to fill the canoe twice.

The wife was amazed as they came in with the first load, and overcome at the sight of the second. The children were excited at the large catch, too. "Did our cousins bring you luck, Daddy?" they asked.

"I guess so," was all he said. He was pleased that they had such vast quantities of fish to prepare and dry. But he did not want his children to become too impressed with the powers of their otter-cousins.

While the woman tended to the fish, the man and his nephews floated the canoe up on high tide, and together they managed to get it above the tide line so that it would not bump against the rocks.

That evening the little otter-nephews were so tired they fell fast asleep by the fire with their tails close to the blaze.

"Your handy little tails are beginning to burn," their uncle teased them.

At these words the otter-nephews were very angry.

"Why do you ridicule us? Is it because we are different from your children?" they cried. Then they jumped up and ran home around the point to their parents.

Early the next day the sister was at the couple's door.

"Why did my little ones run home in the middle of the night? Did something frighten them?" she asked her brother.

"I only teased them that their clothes were going to burn being so close to the fire," the man said altering the truth somewhat to avoid offending his sister. "I am very sorry. I didn't mean to hurt their feelings."

The sister then returned home and passed on the brother's apology. The Land Otter father explained to his children that their uncle was just concerned about their clothes and they agreed to go back. When they returned to their human uncle's place in a few days, they found him getting the canoe ready for his trip home. The man was glad to see that his otter-nephews had returned in good spirits. They helped him load all his provisions into the canoe and then joined the family on the trip back to the village. But when they got close to the town, the husband realized that the three otter-nephews were no longer with him. Nobody had seen them leave.

. Many people were on the beach to greet them when the fisherman and his family returned.

"Where did you get all these provisions?" they asked as they helped unload the shellfish, halibut, and seal.

"Where did you get seal at this time of year?" asked one of the better seal hunters.

"Something really strange happened to us," his wife explained. "We have seen my husband's sister who drowned years ago. She and her Land Otter family helped us." Then she told of the provisions her sister-in-law had brought and the help the otter-nephews had given her husband in fishing.

55

"She must now be a Land Otter Woman living with the Land Otter People," one of the older women said. "What did they look like?"

The woman described her sister-in-law with the round mouth hitched up to her nose and the arms growing out of her breast.

"And hair grew down her back as far as her seat," she said.

"The children had tails," the husband added.

"Those are kushtakas, all right," the old woman said.

"How strange," someone else said. "Kushtakas usually bring bad luck."

"Did they try to lure you to their kingdom?" another asked.

"No," the husband answered. "In fact my nephews rode with me part of the way back to the village." Then he remembered the tail episode.

"My sister once did something strange, though. She sat my children on her lap and sang a song to them. Suddenly I saw them growing tails like her children's. They looked terrible! When I yelled at her to stop, she patted their bottoms and made the tails disappear." Then another thought came to him. "It was surprising how cleverly the otter-children used their tails to get things done quickly." He did not mention the matter of getting the canoe to the water, although he suspected that his otter-nephews had had something to do with it.

The people continued to puzzle over the account of these experiences, but it did not stop them from accepting the gifts of food the husband made to them. The provisions, along with what the people were able to find in shallows and beaches, supplied the villagers for some time.

"Maybe kushtakas aren't all bad," commented one.

"Of course, he did not let his sister get away with changing his children into Land Otter People," an older woman put in. "You always have to keep your guard up with those creatures."

A little later in the spring, when the weather had warmed up a bit, the husband paddled his canoe over to the place where he had gone to fish. The bark house and shed were still there. He went around the point, where his sister had come from, and inspected it carefully for signs of her or his nephews. But no signs of life were to be found — only land otter holes.

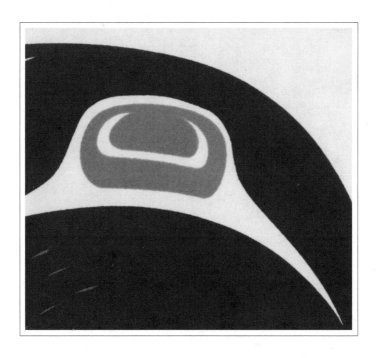

REVENGE

A man of Killsinoo was distraught as his beautiful young wife lay dying. The shaman had been brought in and had donned his medicine-man regalia, shaken his rattles, and done his dance. One by one he had put on the masks of his various spirit aids to implore their help. He had laid an ivory image of the land otter tongue on the patient's body and waited with his long hollow bone to catch the evil spirit as it left her. But all this was in vain. The cure did not work, and neither the shaman nor the girl's family could understand why.

"Could it be a witch's spell that is causing her illness?" the husband asked.

"Who would want to harm such a lovely lady?" the shaman asked in return.

"Maybe I am the one they want to hurt. Maybe somebody begrudges me my luck in hunting or fishing. Or the wealth I have gained from it," the husband mused aloud. "Or perhaps someone envies me my wife. Many other men sought her hand in marriage, but I was the one who won her."

"Witchcraft is a possibility," the shaman said. "I will try to find out whether a witch is involved."

The shaman ordered the chief to call the clan members together. In the meantime he fasted and called upon his spirit powers. By the time the clan members were convened and lined up around the hall, the shaman had reached a trancelike state. One by one, he subjected them to his penetrating stares as, dressed in full regalia, he lingered ominously before each person, waiting for the spirit to identify the guilty one. Witches often betrayed themselves by signs only a shaman could interpret. The clan members in turn shifted nervously, for this was a serious matter. People identified as witches who did not own up to it could be beaten or laid across hot ashes or just left to starve. Or they could be tied to a rock at low tide and left to drown as the tide came in. But after circling the hall several times, the shaman was still unable to detect the presence of a witch.

"A mother and high-caste woman should behave more

properly," some of the women murmured among themselves, "and not be smiling and glancing at other men." Their gossip referred to the chief's son, whom they believed the sick woman favored. The husband's friends occasionally called this to his attention with good-natured teasing.

"Maybe she's been eating berries that have fallen on the ground. They can be tainted by witches," said another, voicing a common belief.

"Oh, she's too good to observe taboos like the rest of us," the first replied. But the men, overhearing this, ignored the women, attributing their remarks to jealousy of the ill wife's good looks.

"Perhaps the witch is from another clan," said one of the relatives. "He could have bewitched a child and persuaded it to bring him her hair or nail clippings or food crumbs." Witches made use of such things, binding them into a ball and placing them inside a recently buried corpse. As the corpse decomposed, the witch's victim became ill, and to effect a cure, the shaman had to identify the witch and have him remove the effigy and destroy it. Anyone who handled the effigy would die, and if it was burned, the patient would die. So identification of the witch was vital.

"A child would also be a possibility," the shaman answered and sent for the sick woman's daughter, the most likely prospect. She could easily have got the personal scraps, since she was often with her mother. And since the child often ran about the village visiting various houses, almost anyone in the village could have bewitched her.

"If you know anything about this, child, tell the shaman," her father said, taking her hand and looking into her large round dark eyes, so like her mother's. "You will not be punished. We just want to know whether **61** anyone asked you to get these things."

"Nobody asked me to do anything," the child insisted.

"Don't be afraid of telling," said the shaman, who was anxious to identify the witch. "It will show that you are innocent. Only a guilty person would hide the truth." But the little girl could only answer "No" or "I don't know" to their questions.

Paralyzed with fear of losing the wife he idolized, the husband kept a vigil by her bed, watching for any change. Even when she was a high-spirited young girl starting to mature, he had noticed her grace and beauty.

"She will make somebody a fine wife some day," he remembered thinking at the time. "Maybe me." So all the while he was distinguishing himself by his expert hunting and fishing, he cherished the hope of someday making her his wife. His hunting and fishing skills had won him a reputation in the village as a good provider and had also made him wealthy. The men saw him as a fine example for the younger boys to imitate, and the women saw him as a good prospect for a husband for their daughters.

The young girl, meanwhile, had reached maturity and become even more beautiful. The uncles of many young men had presented their suits to her family. Among the suitors was the son of one of the highly respected chiefs, a young, handsome man with a winning manner. He had a fine physique, although he was casual about the morning exercise and bathing rituals and lacked the enthusiasm for fishing and hunting that his position as a chief's son required. But his father loved him dearly and was somewhat permissive in his dealing with him.

Though arrangements were made without the presence of the couple to be married, the young woman had learned from gossip that the choice was narrowed to the more mature man and the chief's son. She had hoped it would be the dashing young man, but her fate was in the hands of her mother and uncle. So when they were won over by the older man's reputation and the offer of many coppers and blankets by his uncle, she accepted their decision. She in turn had been rewarded with a rich and adoring husband and a high position in the village.

The husband remembered the events of the marriage day so clearly. She had come in the ermine robe her aunt had made for her, tall and straight, her long black hair hanging down her back and her large black eyes looking somberly at him. It was only during the celebration afterward that her eyes wandered toward the chief's son and twinkled as they met his longing gaze. But her husband was too supremely happy to suspect anything. He had watched this lovely being grow into womanhood and had waited patiently for the day he could ask for her hand. Now she was his to love and she would bear him beautiful children.

After the ceremony and celebration she went to live with her husband in his family house and was a good wife. She bore him a daughter who promised to be as beautiful as she was. But after a few years of marriage, the lively young woman grew bored with her well-ordered life. Occasionally she would exchange a flirtatious glance with the chief's son, and he seemed equally attracted to her. Some of the villagers noticed their little flirtation. The men looked sly and said, "Youth will be youth." But the women murmured, "Nothing good will come of it."

And indeed, their words suddenly seemed to bear weight, for now the young woman was seriously ill, and the shaman seemed unable to cure her. If he could not do so soon, she would die. She appeared to sense this herself.

"My dearest," the sick young woman murmured to her husband. "I know I am dying. Please don't bury me beneath the ground."

"Don't talk of dying, my love. You must get well."

"But if I should die, promise not to bury me. Hang my coffin from a tree until my body is burned. I will suffocate in the ground." Her husband gave her his promise.

He sat by her bed throughout the night and was with her when she died just before morning. Grief-stricken, he bewailed his fate. But in due course he sent for the women from the other clan to prepare her body and lay it in the coffin. When this was done, he gave instructions for the coffin to be put in a tree to await cremation some weeks later.

Each night the bereaved husband visited his wife's remains, staying there for several hours. When he headed for home a little after midnight, the village was in darkness. Only the house of the chief gave off a slight glow from the smoke hole, for he kept a fire burning all night. This had aroused the curiosity of the villagers, who put their fires out each night except for an ember to start anew each morning.

The subject came up one day when the bereaved husband, who had returned to his habit of gambling with friends in the late afternoon, was playing a game of sticks.

"I wonder why the chief has a fire going all night."

"Maybe somebody is sick," another answered.

"But we would have heard."

"Maybe the chief has special guests." But though they questioned one another, they did not learn the reason for the nighttime fire.

The bereaved husband was curious, too. His little girl spent more time than ever visiting from house to house, now that her mother was gone. And the neighbors, who had always enjoyed this charming child, were especially kind to her since her mother's death. Deciding to satisfy his curiosity, the husband woke his daughter up early one morning.

"Our coals have burned out and the house is cold. Run to another house that has a fire going and get me some coals so I can start ours again quickly." The child was dressed in no time and off to do his bidding. As her father expected, the chief's house was the only one with smoke coming from the chimney, and the little girl ran there directly.

"Good morning, little one. What are you doing up so early?" the slave asked as she came to the door.

"My father has sent me for some fire," she answered.

"Everyone is still asleep," said the slave. "Stay here and I'll give you a start."

The child waited by the door as she was told. But she could see people sitting by the fireplace. A man and a woman were talking and laughing. As the woman turned toward her, the child glimpsed her face. It was her mother! But how could it be? Did dead people come back again and live somewhere else? When the woman saw the child, she turned her face away quickly. But seeing something in the movement that was like her mother, the child determined to ask the slave about her.

"Here is your fire, child," said the slave, handing her the coals and hurrying her out the door before she could speak. "There is no time for you to talk now. Your father needs this right away."

The child ran straight home with the fire and gave it **65** to their slave, who set about lighting their fire.

"Where is my father?" the child asked.

"He is out working with his fishing gear," the woman replied.

The child found him on the beach untangling his net. He beamed at her as she came toward him.

"You are back so soon. You didn't stay long." He knew how much she enjoyed visiting with the neighbors.

"I saw my mother this morning," she told him.

"Your mother! Where did you see her?"

"At the chief's house."

"What chief's house?" he asked.

"The chief's house on the hill, the one where the fire burns all night. I went there to get the fire."

"Surely these are just a lonely child's imaginings," the father thought, realizing that the girl must miss her mother terribly.

"You couldn't have seen her, my sweet. Your mother has been dead for some time." Tears came to his eyes as he took the child's hand. "Perhaps you mistook some other woman for your mother."

But the child continued to insist that she had seen her mother.

"Did you talk to this woman?" he asked her.

"No, but I watched her while they got the fire for me. She smiled and moved her head just the way Mother used to." Could the child be under the influence of some supernatural power, the father wondered, or even bewitched, as the shaman had suggested?

"Maybe it was one of your mother's sisters. They look a lot like her. We will visit sometime soon and see." He tried to comfort the child, but he was distressed.

66

What could she have seen?

"Tonight I'll take somebody with me to bring the coffin down, look in, and make sure everything is all right," he said to himself after she had left.

He set out after dark with a companion to the tree where the coffin had been raised off the ground to protect the body from animals while it was kept for cremation. The two men loosened the ropes and started to lower the box slowly.

"The coffin seems lighter," said the companion.

"Maybe the body has dried out somewhat," the husband replied. Certainly his wife's body was in the box, he told himself. Where else could it be? But when they lowered the box to the ground and opened it, it was empty. The husband cried out.

"Where's the body of my wife? Who has stolen it?" the man raged. Gradually some of the good-natured taunts by his friends about the wife's flirtations with the chief's son came back to him. The chief had bartered strongly for the woman's hand for his son before the marriage. Could he have paid a shaman to bring her back to life? But what shaman was powerful enough to do that? The shaman he had sent for could not even keep her from dying, let alone restore her to life. He determined to visit the chief's house in secret to see for himself what his daughter had seen.

He waited at home until after midnight, when all the houses of the village were dark — all except the chief's house on the hill, that is, where a fire burned. He walked up the hill to the house and started to climb the wall. Quietly he worked his way across the roof to the smoke hole and then looked down through it into the house. There before the fire, laughing and talking with the chief's son, **67** sat his dead wife, beautiful as ever in the firelight.

At first his feelings toward her were tender. It was so good to see her lovely face and gentle movements again. The child was right. There was no mistaking her for anyone else. Only she smiled and moved that way. But how did she get there? Did she not die? He remembered her request to have her coffin placed in a tree rather than buried.

Could she have pretended to be ill and then to die? Aspiring shamans, after intense fasting and drinking devil's club juice, had been known to reach a state of trance that was like death. Had she done something similar, using devil's club or other herbs? No wonder the shaman could not find the source of her illness. She and the chief's son must have hatched this plot to get her away from him.

As the husband watched and tried to reconstruct what had happened, he saw the slaves bring food to the couple.

"The others in the house must not know they are there," he thought. "That is why they are being served their food in secret. And that is why the chief has kept a fire burning all night in his house. That man has always doted too much on that boy."

With these thoughts, the husband's joy gradually changed to anger. His wife had feigned illness and death to escape him — to be with the chief's son. How could she have been so cruel to him who loved her so? And how could she have left her little daughter? Did she not miss that beautiful child? Then his thoughts shifted to his own situation.

"This will bring me great humiliation and even ridicule when word gets out," he realized. "I must keep still about it until I decide how to retaliate."

"I will tell my daughter that it was her mother's cousin that she saw," he decided. "They look and act something alike. I will also pay the friend who helped with the coffin to keep quiet. I will give him that blanket he has admired for so long."

All the way back to the village he ruminated on what course to take. Again his anger raged when he thought of the lovers' secret.

"I shall get her back!" he vowed. "I'll kill him for this trickery!" Then as he thought of her infidelity, "I'll kill them both!" His mind was in a turmoil as his feelings went from sorrow to humiliation, jealousy, and rage. The picture of her sitting with the chief's son, smiling — the two of them so happy together — kept returning to torment him.

The husband tossed and turned the whole night, sleeping little. "What can I do?" he raved. At dawn he determined to consult the shaman. He got up and set out for the shaman's dwelling. The shaman too had risen early, as was his habit, and was sitting in the icy water. After gaining the shaman's promise of strict confidence, the husband told his story in a few words.

"My wife is alive," he said.

"But how can that be?" replied the shaman. "I was at her bedside when she died. I wasn't even able to find the cause of her illness."

"She only pretended to take ill and die."

"I don't believe it!"

"I saw her at midnight at the chief's house, sitting near the fire with his son," the husband told him. "They have been enamored of each other for some time, although I never wanted to believe it. They faked her death so she could escape me." Gradually the shaman became convinced of the truth.

"That would explain my failure to find the cause of **69**

her illness. But why would she do that?"

"To deceive me. She is living now at the chief's house with his son. Can you help me? I must punish both of them."

"I was duped by them too," the shaman replied, "and would also like to see them punished. But I have always carried out my duties as a shaman in an honorable way. I cannot visit evil on anybody. Leave them alone. They will soon tire of each other and bring punishment on themselves."

The husband understood the shaman's position. Only witches and wizards visited evil on people and through their evil conjurations caused sickness and death. Shamans were highly regarded for their powers of healing and foretelling the future, all for the good of the community. Witches and wizards, on the contrary, brought harm and bad fortune to people and were despised as outcasts. But the deserted husband was deeply depressed and even desperate. He was unable to accept the shaman's counsel.

"My wife! My wife!" he wailed. "I must get her back." Then he began to rage. "I will avenge this deception. And that cheating son of a chief! I'll kill him!" He continued to pace back and forth in anger, as his desperation became extreme.

"A wizard! That's it! I'll become a wizard." By now he no longer cared what happened to him, or how the other villagers would feel toward him, and gave no thought to his position in the community. He could see no further than his own present grief and anger. The discovery of his wife's deception had destroyed his peace, and he could not rest until he had had his revenge and restored his honor.

70   The husband went out to the graveyard, where he

knew the witches used to go, and like them, dug around the bodies and played with the bones in order to make himself a wizard. But he felt no special powers come to him. Then the overwrought husband threw caution to the winds. He paddled out to the island across the bay from the village where the dead shamans' bodies were sent, since they were not cremated, and played with the bones there. This was not only a desecration of the dead but also was very dangerous, as handling even the possessions of a shaman could cause insanity or death. But this desperate act was believed to produce the powers of witchcraft.

For several more days the husband roamed without food or sleep. Finally, in the grave of one of the shamans, he found a man's shoulder blades still connected. He took them in his hands and worked them back and forth. Then he fanned himself with them and rubbed them against his own shoulder blades. Suddenly he fell into a faint.

When he came to, it seemed to him that the shoulder blades he had found in the graveyard were fixed to his own back. He tried working them like wings, and they flapped back and forth. Soon he found himself flying through the air, gaining speed as he went. It was a dizzying sensation. He felt detached from his body, which was floating weight-lessly in the air. In no time he was circling over the house of the chief's son.

"Hold on," he said to himself. "First I must make some weapons," and headed for the woods. There he found some small limbs of hardwood, which he split into tiny shafts about the size of gambling sticks. He shaped the ends into points, dipped them in grease, and then rotated them in the fire to harden them.

Then he found himself flying again, the wings still

attached at his shoulder blades and flapping vigorously, the dartlike weapons in his hand. He landed on the roof of the chief's house and waited for evening. When it was dark and all had gone to sleep for the night, he cast a sleeping spell on the guards at the door and then flew down the smoke hole. Amazed at his new-found power to bewitch, he started with the low-caste relatives sleeping nearer the door and on the lower circles around the fire and worked his way to the back where the higher ranks slept, casting a spell over all to keep them from waking. Finally he came to his wife and the chief's son lying together behind the screen.

"Ah, there you are!" he roared, startling them awake. Aghast at the sight of his mistress's husband, the chief's son began to plead for his life.

"Hold your hand, old man! We can settle this peacefully. My father has stores of blankets and copper shields he will give you if you spare my life. Then you will be able to win a younger wife."

The deserted husband shuddered with rage at this suggestion. "Your plan was clever but your deeds were vile. Only death will vindicate you." With these words he flung a dart into the young man's breast.

The fickle wife looked on in horror at this spectacle, knowing that her turn was coming. Only briefly did her husband hesitate as he looked on her beautiful, stricken face. But his heart was hardened to love and compassion, and he felt only rage at the humiliation she had caused him. He sent the other dart into her breast and left unseen through the smoke hole. Then he was aware of nothing more.

When the husband awoke the next morning, he was still on the island in the shaman's graveyard and felt as though he had been in a wrestling match. "What am I doing here?" he wondered. Then in his numb state, he staggered to his canoe, launched it, and headed for the village.

Meanwhile, the village had begun to buzz with rumor and gossip, for at first light, the chief's son and his mistress had been found dead near the fireplace. The fire that had burned throughout the night for many months had gone out.

"Why did you let the fire go out? Did you fall asleep?" the stunned villagers asked the servants. They explained that they had wakened from a deep sleep toward morning to find the fire out. They started it again from the embers and then got ready to serve the young couple.

"When it was almost dawn and they had not appeared, we thought we should waken them," one said.

"When we went behind the screen, we found them lying together," another said. "It was only as we got closer that we could see blood flowing from their mouths."

"Then we saw the small darts," the first one continued, "and ran screaming for the chief and his wife."

When the boy's parents were told the awful news, they too had cried out in shock and grief at the loss of their son.

"This is all my fault," the chief wailed. "I should not have helped them in their deceit. But they were so young and so much in love, I could not bear to part them. And I loved my son too much to send him away."

At the same time the wife was also ranting. "Who has done this? Who has done this?" she cried over and over, running back and forth and tearing her hair. "We have all been punished. O my son! My son!" The slaves and her friends tried without success to quiet her.

Nor did the people of the village know what to make of the tragedy. The men were on the beach stocking the fishing boats with nets and hooks. Farther up the beach lay the longer war canoes, their painted bows gleaming in the sun. One of the women had run down to the men with the news.

"Did someone come from outside, or did one of the chief's relatives kill them?" asked one of the men as they were heading up to the house.

"How could anyone get in?" asked another. "The doors were guarded."

"The guards said they never went to sleep before serving the young couple," the woman explained. "They don't know what happened this time."

"Maybe a witch cast a spell on the guards to get by them and then on the others to keep them from waking up."

"I thought she had died," said one. "How did she return to life?"

"Maybe the chief's son was a wizard," someone answered.

"Can they bring people back to life?" someone else asked.

On the edge of the crowd, the dead woman's husband, after beaching his boat, came into view. The curious onlookers turned toward him.

"Did you see your wife?" they asked. "She was with the chief's son." "She's been stabbed." "Did you know she was alive?" "How did she come back to life?" Questions and comments poured out one after the other and some at the same time.

"My wife died some time ago," he was finally able to answer. "I know nothing about this."

The chief ordered one of the men to call in the women from the other clan to wash the bodies and lay them out for burial. The preparation for the funeral rites began.

In the meantime the excitement died down somewhat and the men returned to their afternoon gambling. The deserted husband was among them. When it was his turn to play, he shouted out to distract the players as all gamblers do. But people wondered at what he was saying.

"These are sharp sticks. These are sharp sticks," he kept repeating. He was smiling slightly and there was a far-away look on his face. Slowly he began to sort out the hazy recollections of the events of the previous night.

Had they really happened? He could hardly remember going to the island, let alone returning to the village or any actions afterwards. When he had awakened in the morning, he had been lying beside the shaman's grave. The shoulder-blade wings were on the ground beside him. Had it all been a dream? Or had he been bewitched? People were often unconscious of their acts while bewitched. Maybe the spirits of the dead shaman had used him to punish the young couple.

To the villagers also, the deaths of the couple remained a mystery. What spirit power had intervened to see that justice was done? With the punishment of the errant lovers, the husband's honor had been restored. But his friends noticed a change in him. As he huddled over his gambling sticks, a cryptic smile and preoccupied air tempered his usual enthusiasm. Should he play the crab or the devilfish?

"These are very sharp sticks," he would say as he deliberated.

DEAD MAN'S BRIDE

Ayoung girl who was just out of seclusion was walking along the beach with one of her aunts. She was still pale and tired easily from her recent lack of sunshine and exercise. Like all young girls coming into maturity, she had been secluded behind a screen in the house and for months had seen no one but her mother, aunt, and a female servant. Their conversations concerned only her instruction and her daily routine. She had no idea of what was going on in the family or the community.

Now that she had come out of seclusion, she was being kept away from men while her aunt and uncle arranged a marriage for her. She had observed her ritual faithfully. It had been months since she had even talked with her friends, many of whom were in seclusion too. She was eager to see her favorite cousin, who was also due to come out soon. They had grown up together and had had their ear-piercing ceremony at the same party. The cousin was as spirited and unpredictable as the chief's daughter was sedate and docile. The aunt had hoped the chief's daughter would be a good influence on her less manageable cousin.

"Have any suitors come to see my mother and uncle?" she asked her aunt as they sat on a log to rest.

"Oh, there have been a few," her aunt teased with a sideward glance. As the daughter of the chief of the village, this girl was actually sought after by many high-caste men as a bride for one of their nephews.

"Did his uncle come?" she asked, alluding to the son of one of the other chiefs. Her companion's face dropped.

"Oh child, of course you didn't hear! It happened while you were in seclusion. He and his brother did not return from a fishing trip."

"You mean they drowned?" cried the girl.

"Their boat was found overturned in the water, but they were never found." The girl, sad to hear this news, wept quietly. She had hoped their families would arrange her marriage with this particular young man. Although a high-born girl did not talk to young men before marriage, these two had glanced at each other appreciatively on occasion, before her seclusion.

"Don't cry, child. There are many fine young men who would like you for their bride," her aunt assured her. But the joy had gone out of the sunny day for the girl.

"Let's go back now," she said. As they got close to the house, she tripped on something underfoot and bent to pick it up. Realizing it was a human skull, she drew back quickly.

"Who on earth has been putting skulls in front of our house?" she asked and shoved it into the brush with her foot.

"Don't touch it!" said her aunt. "Someone could be putting a curse on you." They became frightened and hurried indoors.

That night, after she had been asleep for some time, the young woman saw two young men coming toward her. "I must be dreaming," she thought. For one was the man she had favored, who had disappeared at sea, and the other was his brother.

"You have come back. You didn't die after all," she cried, and in the optimism that sprang from this dream-like state, she assumed the man she had earlier hoped would ask for her hand in marriage had come to claim her, and she became his wife.

When she awoke the next morning, she was amazed to find this dream-husband in bed with her, and his brother sleeping next to him. At the same time a servant, who had been sent to waken her, came in and found the girl talking to someone supposedly lying next to her.

"Look, here is my husband!" the girl said. But the servant, who could see only an indentation on the pillow, bolted from the room and ran back to the girl's mother.

"Your daughter says she's married!" she cried. "She **79**

says she's married and looks at someone next to her in bed. But nobody's there!"

"Married? But how could that be?" the startled mother asked. "She didn't know any men. Her aunt has been with her all the time."

While her mother and the servant were still discussing the matter, the daughter came in to breakfast and presented her good-looking husband. The mother, dumbstruck, could only gape at them as they sat down to breakfast. Everyone else was staring, too. For all they could see was a human skull floating beside the girl at head height. They had never seen anything like this before, though some had heard strange stories that this type of thing happened when someone returned from the Land of the Dead.

Unaware of their predicament, the girl carried on an ordinary conversation with the unseen man she called her husband, who was asking for a small canoe and hunting equipment. But only she could hear him.

"Mother, my husband would like to use the small canoe and some spears and arrows. He wants to go hunting with his brother." Since nobody could see anything to indicate the presence of the brother, they assumed that the husband would meet him some place.

Not knowing what else to do, the mother decided to humor her daughter. If the unseen husband and his brother went hunting, she would have the girl alone and could talk to her. The slaves went out to look for the canoe where it had been beached, but it was gone. When the girl relayed this news to her husband, it did not seem to trouble him. He and his brother promptly sat down on the floor in the middle of the room and went through the motions of paddling a canoe, to the horror and embarrassment of the young woman, who didn't realize that nobody else could see them. The two men continued their charade, going through the motions of sighting seal and spearing them.

"Let's camp," the husband then suggested to his brother. They went outside and pulled some of the painted boards off the side of the girl's father's house to start a fire and then set rocks on the blaze to heat so they could cook some of their catch. Only the girl could see or hear all this activity, which kept them busy until late in the evening, when they paddled home again. When she saw them appearing to struggle under the weight of the seal, the girl called to her mother for help.

"Mother, my husband and his brother have returned with a loaded canoe. They are bringing things up and need some help."

"There's a canoe on the beach," the mother said to the slaves, intending to humor her daughter further. For to all of them the invisible husband seemed to have stayed in the house by the fire — or at least the skull did. "The men need help carrying the catch up to the house."

When the slaves went out as directed, they found the canoe that was missing earlier now tied up at the shore, full of all kinds of fish, seal, and sea lions.

"I don't know where these came from," the girl's father said. "But we can certainly use them." He gave a seal to the head man of each family and was able to feed the whole village with the rest of the catch.

The following week a large supply of game was found at the doorstep of the girl's house. There were bear, goats, deer, and groundhogs.

"Your new husband has brought us good fortune," said the father. "We are lucky to have so much fresh

81

fish and meat through his skill."

As the mysterious supplies of food continued to appear in the village, the people, who had at first been wary of the strange visitors that only the chief's daughter could see, began to hold them in highest regard. By this time the skull of the other man had appeared. Now both shadowy bodies could be made out, attached to the skulls the people had seen originally. Gradually the two men began to take on a more solid shape and to look familiar to the villagers.

"Aren't these the two men who drowned last year?" asked one of the men.

"They do look like the chief who lost his two sons," another agreed.

"Maybe they are Land Otter Men," added a third. But the people did not want to think that. Although Land Otter People were known to be friendly on occasion, they were generally associated with trickery and death. But these men did not have the elongated otterlike bodies of the "slim men" who had become kushtakas.

Finally, after some time, the two men became entirely visible to all people. Only then did their father, the chief of his house, dare to believe that his two sons had come back. During their lives they had been great hunters and fishermen, exemplary sons of a chief. Now they were even better at their work, supplying the entire village with provisions. Their father embraced them and welcomed them back into the family.

The head chief, the girl's father, brought out two magnificent ermine robes and placed one over the shoulders of each of the men. He accepted the husband as his true son-in-law and welcomed both men into the family with these **82** handsome gifts. The villagers, too, began to believe they were ordinary people and accepted the man and woman as husband and wife.

"The people owe you many thanks for the supplies of goods you have brought us," he said. "You have been very generous to the entire village. Please honor us by continuing to live in this house." The men accepted his offer graciously and continued to be good providers.

The high-spirited cousin of the new bride was amazed at the turn of events. She had been enamored of the younger brother before his supposed death and now wanted more than ever to be his wife. A close friend of the bride's, she had many opportunities to gain his attention. She made a point of sitting near him at dinner, listening intently to the stories he told. She tried in many other ways to get him to notice her, but he appeared to have no time for her. He was from a family of wealth and high status, and such people believed that a young woman should be reserved and behave modestly. Until marriage, a well-reared young woman did not speak to men, and those of high status kept away from them entirely. It was up to the mother and uncle to choose a suitable husband for her.

This cousin, a very pretty girl, was not so conscientious about these observances as she should have been. In fact, she thought they were rather silly and so did not hesitate to take matters into her own hands.

"Why don't you put in a good word for me with your brother-in-law?" she asked her cousin one day. Since their seclusion the two girls were still friendly, although the bride was gentle and quietly observed custom and proper behavior as carefully as possible while her lively cousin believed rules were to be challenged and was always up to some kind of mischief. The two did not see each other as **83** often as formerly, since the bride's wifely duties took more of her time.

"I'll do my best," the young wife promised. "But you know how serious my brother-in-law is. He might find your high spirits too much for him."

"Oh, he'll come round when he sees that obeying the rules isn't all there is to life," she answered with a taunting look. She enjoyed teasing her demure cousin.

When the young man continued to put off her advances, the cousin was not happy. She began to think that perhaps the bride had not pleaded her case as strongly as she wished.

"She probably doesn't want to share all that glory with anyone else," she said to herself. For by now the wonders the young men performed were the talk of the village and had brought honor to both families. As the wife of one, the bride received a good share of the adulation, a source of envy to the more outgoing cousin.

At their next meeting, she approached the bride in an accusatory tone. "Your brother-in-law hasn't been any friendlier to me," she said. "What did you say to him?"

Startled at her cousin's hostile manner, the bride replied, "He changed the subject right away whenever I mentioned you."

"You could not have tried very hard," her cousin came back. "Maybe you are enjoying having all that honor for yourself."

Taken aback by this outburst, the bride could only protest that she had done her best.

"Besides, who is he to brush me off?" the cousin added, smarting at the young man's apparent rebuff.

84　　"Maybe he disapproves of your trying to get his

attention," suggested the bride, as she regained her composure. "Men of high caste like a woman to behave more properly."

"So your relatives feel superior to me! Well, I come from a family of high status, too." And she huffed off. But in the days that followed, while managing to remain outwardly friendly to the couple, the bride's cousin set about finding a way to soothe her hurt pride.

She knew that people who returned from the dead had a precarious hold on life. Various things, such as human blood or rattling bones, could send them back to the Land of the Dead. Then an idea came to her.

The next day she greeted her cousin with an exuberance that concealed the coolness she had begun to feel even before their recent heated exchange. The young married woman was happy to see her cousin cheerful and pleasant again. When they were getting the food ready for dinner that night, the cousin offered to help. Then, while filleting the fish, she purposely nicked her thumb with the knife and squeezed out of few drops of blood. Unseen she rubbed her bloody thumb on the seat where the young man she desired usually sat for dinner. The bride noticed her trying to stop the bleeding.

"Did you cut yourself?" she asked.

"I just nicked my thumb with the knife," the cousin came back quickly.

"And you're the one who's so good at filleting," said the bride, smiling. "Is something distracting you?" The others working around them laughed, too.

The men were in high spirits as they came in for dinner, having had a good day fishing. They sat in their usual places to eat and were joking and telling stories, when

85

they noticed the younger brother fading into a shadow.

"What's happening, Brother?" asked the girl's husband, reaching over to grab his arm. But the young man kept on fading until he disappeared entirely. The people were terrified.

"Where did he go?" asked one.

"Who knows?" another said. "Maybe back to the Land of the Dead."

"Do you think he and his brother came from there?"

"What made him leave so suddenly?"

The remaining brother was inconsolable, for the two men had been inseparable since their accident. His bride tried in vain to comfort him. She, too, was sad to lose her brother-in-law, whom she had grown to like very much, and she was afraid something similar might happen to her husband. The men's father was heartbroken too, but took comfort in having the older son with him still.

The husband continued to hunt and fish but without his earlier enthusiasm. The girl was saddened by his persisting sorrow and worried about the distance she felt growing between them. She confided in her cousin, who pretended to offer sympathy.

"Maybe I can cheer him up," her cousin suggested, only too willing to get into the good graces of the husband, maybe even win him for herself. She was jealous of the bride, who still had a highly prized husband, while she now had no one even to raise her hopes. She was not satisfied with the trouble she had already caused, and the success of her treachery made her even more brazen.

Under the pretense of cheering him up, she flirted openly with the husband. But he shrank from her. Something inside him seemed to connect her with his brother's death. Stung by the husband's coldness toward her, she determined that he should meet the same fate as his brother. Again she approached the bride with the friendly concern and offered to help with dinner.

"I'm sorry I couldn't get your husband on a happier track," she said. "You will just have to wait for him to get over his grief." Then as she helped prepare the food, again she marked the place where the husband would sit with blood from her pricked finger.

"Did you cut yourself again?" the bride asked, seeing her cousin wiping the blood from her finger.

"You are getting clumsy," said one of the aunts.

When the husband came in, sober and preoccupied, he sat in his usual place for dinner. Then while everyone was talking and eating, he, too, began to shrink gradually to a shadow and finally disappeared entirely.

Again the people of the village were greatly frightened and did not know what to make of these occurrences.

"Now both men have returned to the Land of the Dead," was the accepted verdict. But even in her grief, the bride noticed a strange look on her cousin's face.

"I wonder if she had something to do with the disappearances of my husband and his brother," she mused. Reviewing in her mind the cousin's actions shortly before the two men's deaths, she remembered her "accidents" with the knife. Each accident had happened before the evening meal at which each man died.

"Blood," she thought. "I wonder if she managed to get some blood on the men." Then an even worse thought occurred to her. "That would be witchcraft!" But she dismissed that thought quickly. "My cousin could not be a witch."

But a coldness grew between the two, once such close friends. No longer welcome in the chief's house, the cousin lost standing in the community and ended by marrying into a household of much lower status than her family had enjoyed.

LDAXIN THE SKEPTIC

AT the beach, Ldaxin the young hunter was getting ready to go out on a seal hunt, and his younger brothers were helping to load his boat. As he was about to leave, dark clouds appeared to the southeast.

"Looks like there might be rain. Are you sure you should be going out?" asked one of the brothers. "Dad and our uncles are waiting to see what the weather will be."

"I can duck into a cove if a storm comes up," he replied.

"Ldaxin can handle anything," teased the younger brother, giving him a friendly shove. Ldaxin raised his arm in a mock gesture of hitting him. His manner was easy but assured.

"I always come in with a good catch, don't I, Little Brother?" The youngest had to agree. Ldaxin was highly regarded by the villagers for his hunting and fishing skills, which brought a good supply of meat and fish for all of them.

"Watch out for kushtakas," said the youngest, mimicking Ldaxin's grandmother. They all laughed.

"Kushtakas!" said Ldaxin. "Has your grandmother been filling your head with silly stories?" The women were full of kushtaka stories, which they embroidered with relish to warn children not to go too far into the woods or into the water. Most of the men believed a little in kushtakas, but the younger ones tended to have their doubts about them. Women could concern themselves with such imaginings, Ldaxin felt, but men had to concentrate on the necessities for survival. Though he made light of kushtakas with his older brother, the youngest boy was not sure how he felt about them.

"I've seen people brought back from the woods or beach, rescued from kushtakas. The shaman helps find them."

"The shaman! He's an old man who dances and sings songs," Ldaxin said, launching into a comic imitation of a shaman dance. Even these casual movements revealed his powerful muscles. "He can deal with them in his way, and I'll deal with them in mine."

"But have you heard the stories people who are rescued tell?"

"About the 'slim men' with short arms growing out of their chests and their lips pulled up under their noses?" Ldaxin asked. "Sure, they 'talk excited.'"

"Grandma says they can imitate the voices of people's relatives and trick people into going with them," the youngest went on seriously.

"Well, I'll be careful," Ldaxin said with a smile and jumped lightly into the boat.

"Good luck, and bring back lots of seals," the middle brother called, as they pushed his canoe away from shore. He would have loved to go with Ldaxin, but both younger boys had to go fishing with their father in the larger family canoe. Ldaxin could go out alone because he had proven his skills as boatman and hunter, for as the oldest, he had had special training from his uncle, one of the best.

Ldaxin enjoyed getting off by himself on the water, especially on a soft day like this. The sky was streaked with thin clouds, the sun shining hazily through them. The water was flat and reflected the dull blue of the sky. His canoe skimmed easily along, and in a few hours he had reached the rocks where the seals made their home.

Ldaxin was a good hunter. As he circled to the dark side of the rock behind the spot where the seals were sunning themselves, he gave it wide berth so they would not see or hear his boat approach. He looked for a good foothold and then jumped, his club in one hand and the bow line of his canoe in the other. He secured the line around a point of rock and crawled toward the sunny side, careful to avoid cutting himself on the sharply etched,

91

barnacled surfaces. He stood awhile surveying his prey. He knew he would have a chance at only one or two seals, for with the first disturbance, the others would slide into the water and dive deep.

"That big one fairly close looks good," he thought. "And there's another in that group farther away. They might not be alerted as quickly to what's happening."

He stole up behind the first big seal and clubbed it on the head. Then he got two small ones on his way to the second big one before the rest had disappeared into the water. Four in all. He was a good hour loading his catch into the canoe, working carefully not to damage the fur or bruise the flesh. The fur would make many capes, and the inner skins would be sewn into clothing. Even the intestines would be put to use. The flesh, of course, would be used for food or oil. Nothing would be wasted.

When Ldaxin was ready to set off for home again, he noticed that the dark clouds he had seen earlier looked more threatening.

"Could be a storm coming up. I had better get going." Ldaxin decided against stopping at the many stream outlets along the shore to see how the fish were doing, not wanting to get caught in a storm with his heavy load.

When he was about a third of the way home, the storm hit. At first the waves were deep but manageable. But soon they became violent, tossing the small craft about so that not even Ldaxin's expert paddling could keep it on course. Finally the boat capsized, throwing him into the sea. He was stunned at first but got his bearings and swam to the overturned craft. He pulled himself up onto the hull and lay across it to ride the waves, hoping somebody would come along to rescue him.

When Ldaxin did not return that night, his family thought he might have gone into a cove to ride out the storm. But after several days passed and the storm had blown itself out, they became alarmed. His brothers and cousins set out in canoes to look for him but could find no sign of him on the water or the beaches. There was only one conclusion. The kushtakas must have captured him.

"We must consult the shaman," Ldaxin's uncle said at the end of the fourth day. "If the kushtakas have him, we must hurry to try to rescue him."

"Kushtakas! Huh!" the middle brother scoffed. "He's probably beached somewhere."

"Ldaxin is too strong-willed to give in to the kushtakas," the youngest brother said quickly, trying to cover up his brother's comment. But the uncle caught it.

"Kushtakas can work in strange ways to overpower even strong-willed people who refuse to go with them," he explained, with a stern look in the middle brother's direction. "Their presence can make people drowsy and too numb to defend themselves. We had better call in the shaman."

When Ixt the shaman arrived, the uncle made him a handsome offering to find the lost man, and the shaman accepted it. He ordered the fire lit and food prepared for him to throw into it at the proper time. In the meantime, he would fast for a day and take a purification bath before the ceremony.

Before the ritual began, the women were sent out to avoid contaminating the shaman or preventing contact with the spirits by their presence. He began to sing his spirit songs and dance around the fire. From outside, the women could hear the goings-on, and one

93

of them peeked through a crack.

"He's letting his hair down. It reaches to the floor!" she told the others. Then she started to scream, but one of the other women clapped a hand over her mouth.

"Shh! They'll hear you."

"His hair! It's alive! I saw it dancing around him," she gasped when they released her. One of the other women looked through the crack.

"It looks like snakes!" she cried.

With each song the shaman threw dried salmon or seal meat onto the fire and asked a spirit for help. Finally he was able to see Ldaxin.

"Ldaxin is not in trouble. He is on the beach sleeping under his canoe. He has caught many seals." The men were glad to hear this news, but they still did not know where he was.

"Send your spirits to help him. Keep the kushtakas away from him," the uncle said. The shaman took up his songs and dances again.

Though he did not know it, Ldaxin needed their help, for he had been up against the kushtakas from the time he took hold of his overturned canoe. After he had been in the water a long while, he saw a boat approaching. The people looked familiar, like relatives, but their bodies and heads were disproportionately long.

"There's my mother's sister! But what is she doing here?" Ldaxin remembered that she had drowned some time ago.

"Kushtakas! This must be what people see." He turned away and looked again. The boat was nowhere in sight.

"Hallucination! That's what I thought."

But as he and his canoe floated on the water, the illusion returned. Long-deceased relatives appeared, reaching out their hands to pull him into their canoe. But he clung stubbornly to the boat.

Ldaxin had no idea how much time had passed since his boat overturned, but he must have fallen asleep, for he awoke dazed and numb with cold on a rocky beach. His canoe had washed up, too, with most of his catch still lashed to it. He pulled himself over to the boat and crawled under it before losing consciousness again.

It was dark when the rapping on the canoe began. Then he heard what sounded like his mother's voice.

"We have been worrying about you for many nights."

"Come on inside to rest now," his father seemed to be saying. "It is cold and damp outside." He tried to lift himself up to look outside, but his arms were heavy with exhaustion, and he could raise his head just a little. He looked around but could see nobody. So he remained prostrate under the boat, his mind on the unusual sounds that continued to reach his ears. Could these be kushtakas? Was something protecting him from them? Then he drifted into oblivion again.

The kushtakas continued their mischief off and on. During the day he was able to catch glimpses of them, or at least their shadowy forms. Once he reached for his gun, but his arms were too heavy and numb to be of much use. His visitors went on making offers of help, but he kept refusing them.

The constant patting on the canoe kept Ldaxin from sleeping much. A second time he was able to raise himself and look outside the canoe, but still he could see nothing. The darkness hid the kushtakas' shadowy forms. The only

95

evidence of their presence was the heaviness of his arms and legs and the drowsiness he had to fight off — and the ceaseless knocking on the canoe.

"My imagination! I am going crazy, I guess, being out so long by myself." Then he lay down again under the canoe and somehow managed to drop off to sleep.

Finally the shaman was able to identify the place where Ldaxin was beached and sent his uncles and brothers in a large canoe to help him. Following the shaman's directions, the rescue party found the beach and spotted the boat.

"There is his canoe," said the youngest brother, pointing to a cove along the shore. They hurried ashore and ran toward the boat. When Ldaxin heard the commotion, he thought the mischief-makers were returning. This time he was able to work the gun loose and fire a few shots. But he was still dazed and weak, and his aim was poor. Once the rescuers got closer to him, they were able to grab hold of him and carry him down to the boat. At the same time he became convinced that this time his visitors were friends.

As they were loading Ldaxin into the boat, his uncle and brothers could feel a fuzziness on his skin, a light furriness.

"Kushtaka defilement!" said the uncle. "The shaman will remove that."

"Do you believe that?" Ldaxin muttered in his semiconscious state. He was still not sure the kushtaka incidents had not been just his delirious imagining. But he could not make himself wake up, and his arms and legs felt furry.

As soon as they landed, they took Ldaxin to the shaman and laid his semiconscious body on the bench by the fire. After washing him, the women were dismissed, and the shaman began the purification ceremonies. He sang his spirit songs and danced around the fire, and then rubbed the young man's body with mud, murmuring incantations. Gradually Ldaxin became lucid and his strength began to return.

"Could this old medicine man have saved me from delirium and death?" he wondered. He now realized that he had almost died of exhaustion and exposure.

"How did you know where to find me?" he asked his middle brother.

"Father had Ixt the shaman call on his spirits to find you and help you to battle the kushtakas."

"Kushtakas! That is who must have been knocking on my canoe."

"Your arms and legs were furry when we found you. You were almost lost to them." Ldaxin shuddered at the reminder of the furry skin, believed to be the first stage of changing into a kushtaka. He remembered the "slim men" and the shadowy forms he had seen. Though they had pounded on his canoe, they didn't come after him. Could the shaman's songs have protected him? He now regretted ridiculing the old man and the dance and ritual, especially in front of his youngest brother.

The next day was clear and bright, and it was hard to believe there had ever been a storm. Ldaxin went to work making repairs to his damaged canoe, which had been towed in behind the family boat. His youngest brother came over to help him.

"Did you really see kushtakas?" he asked.

"Well, something a lot like them, I guess," Ldaxin replied. "You had better listen to your grandmother. She knows what is right. And keep up your ritual baths and exercises."

One of the cousins working on his boat nearby tried to get a reaction from Ldaxin. "Here's the man rescued from the kushtakas."

"If you say so," Ldaxin replied quietly. That was not the answer his cousin expected. Where was the old cocksure Ldaxin? This fellow wasn't going to be much fun.

Not far from them the women sat skinning and filleting the seals and discussing the events of the last few days as they worked.

"I guess Ldaxin got a real scare from those kushtakas," one of them said.

"I bet he's not so sure they don't exist now," said another.

"He's lucky to be here," said a third. "He's lucky we have such a good shaman."

"That shaman didn't only get Ldaxin back," another cackled. "He brought back all his catch, too!"

It took the women most of the day to cut the meat and render the oil. They were able to fill many storage boxes to put away for the winter.

XAT AND THE FEATHER KITE

HIS real name was Xat-cugu'lk!i, but they called him Xat. He seemed a normal sort of boy as he played along the beach.

But there was a mystery in his beginnings. Not long before he was born, his grandmother had told him, all the people of the village disappeared, even the men who hewed out canoes on the outskirts of town. Only his mother and grandmother, who had been gathering spruce roots deep in the forest at the time, remained. When they returned, they were amazed to find the village empty.

"Where could everyone be?" the older woman asked in amazement.

"The boats are still here," said the daughter. "I'll go up to the house." But she found nobody, either there or at the site where men hollowed canoes.

It was only years later, after Xat's heroic feat, that they learned the story of the disappearance. It seems that while the women had been gone, the rest of the people were down on the beach — the men getting their boats ready for fishing, the women helping to stock them, and the children playing — when out of nowhere a large plume, seemingly from an enormous bird, floated down. The children were the first to run out and reach up for it. Thinking it was another toy, they left off playing and, without asking permission, went after it. One of the boys jumped and grasped it, and it carried him skipping along the beach, lifting him off the ground a little, every third or fourth hop. The others thought this was funny and ran to take hold of him. But as one child grabbed him, the first was lifted into the air, so that the second was left with his feet only occasionally touching the ground. The children, of course, found this great fun. They laughed and cheered as each child took the feet of the lowest and the others went ever higher into the sky. The women, busy with their work, finally noticed the commotion.

"My gosh, look at the children!" one woman

screamed, as they floated by, looking like the knotted tail

of a kite. Far, far into the sky they could see what looked like a plume.

"How did they get up there?" asked another, as they both ran toward the last child, who was holding the feet of the one above him. The other women hastily set down their baskets of food and hurried after them toward the kite tail.

The first woman grabbed the child to bring him down, but she was lifted off the ground. The next grabbed her and she, too, started up. One by one the women tried to pull the plume and its load to earth, until all had ascended with it. The men, who usually left the management of the children to the women, had been slower to act. Now they, too, cast aside their paddles and spears and ran toward the dangling string of people in the sky. But they were no more successful in bringing the others down. Finally the canoe builders, who had heard the hullaballoo from the outskirts of town where they were working, abandoned their partially hollowed logs and adzes and came to see what it was all about. There were all the people of the village strung up into the sky on a strange plume and shouting for help. Finally the builders also grasped the feet of the last man, but even their greater strength did not keep them from the fate of the others. By the time Xat's mother and grandmother returned from the woods, the whole phenomenon had drifted out of sight.

The two remaining women carried on by themselves, catching enough fish at the mouth of the streams and gathering berries enough to keep them from hunger in season and out.

Xat's grandmother had been famous throughout all the villages for the fine weave and artistry of her spruce root baskets and ceremonial hats. Her skills required a strong respect for their culture and ritual, which many of the other villagers lacked. As was the custom, the grandmother had kept her daughter by her side while she worked, so the young woman could learn the skill and carry on the tradition.

Even now, alone in the village, they continued to make their baskets. They first had to gather the roots and prepare them, going into the woods to cut roots from the base of the spruce trees and then soften them in water on their return to the village. But often the girl would soften some of the roots by chewing them. She swallowed some of the juice at first by accident, and then on purpose, because she liked its sweet taste. Next she began chewing up the finer roots and swallowing them. Her uncle had told her that spruce root juice had special powers. Soon she began to feel a baby forming within her. She wondered at this strange happening, but continued to chew the roots. When the child was born, she called him Xat-cugu'lk!i, Root-stump.

It was a lonely existence for the little boy, with no other children to play with, but he amused himself along the beach and caught fish in the stream. When he was old enough, his grandmother showed him how to make a tight circle of rocks between the low and high tide lines for a fish trap. When the tide was high, the circle would fill with fish, which would be trapped in the little rock-edged pond when the tide went out. As he grew older, it was his job to catch the fish while the women filleted them and hung the strips to dry. They stored the cured fish in boxes for provisions when the fishing season was over.

The boy Xat also went with them to pick berries: red and blue huckleberries, yellow and red salmonberries, wild strawberries and cranberries, and soapberries. The last were often whipped until frothy and used as a dessert cream. He learned to hunt beaver and porcupines and even got an occasional deer.

At the same time Xat's mother saw that he kept the morning rituals of bathing in the icy water, switching himself with twigs afterwards, and drinking devil's club juice. These routines were observed to strengthen him and keep him clean, so he would be ready when his clan spirit chose to come to him. Discipline and cleanliness were important to the spirits.

Xat's grandmother passed the family heritage on to him by telling him the clan legends. Some of his favorite heroes were Natsilane, who created the beautiful killer whales, and brave Gunhar, who went to the Killer Whale kingdom under the sea to rescue his captured wife. But Blackskin, whose likeness was carved on one of the posts of the clan house, was closest to him. He gazed often in admiration at the figure holding the huge sea lion up by the tail, having ripped its body in half lengthwise. The story of Blackskin's rise to power and fame appealed to Xat.

This hero was called Blackskin because of his dirty appearance, which came from lying in the soot close to the fire. He also seemed to sleep more than the rest of the boys, since he did not get up in the morning to bathe with them or take part in their strength-building contests. So he was considered lazy and weak as well as dirty.

Xat enjoyed the thought of Blackskin's fooling his family, especially his two bullying older brothers, when he would steal out at night and sit in the icy water longer than even the full-grown men did in the mornings. Then he would flog himself with branches, drink devil's club juice, and go back to bed before the others stirred.

Xat tensed as his grandmother told of Blackskin's wrestling matches with Strength-of-the-North-Wind, where at first he was wrestled to the ground by Strength but was eventually able to beat him. After that victory, Strength took Blackskin to the trees where the other young men of the village tested their strength daily. After bathing and switching one another, the men would run first to an old tree at one end of the village and try to dislodge a new limb growing from it. Then they would race to a young spruce at the other end of the village and try to twist it to the root. None of them ever succeeded at either task. But on his first attempt Blackskin dislodged the new limb, twisted the young spruce, and then carefully put them in place again. When Blackskin's brothers were also able to accomplish these feats the next morning, not knowing what their brother had done the night before, they thought they were ready to hunt the mammoth sea lion that had killed their uncle with a flap of his tail. But it was Blackskin, of course, who was the strong man, and after his two brothers died in the attempt, he tore the huge sea lion in two.

"You need to work at becoming strong and to keep clean so you will be ready for your spirit powers when they come to you," his grandmother told Xat. "And respect our traditions even when they seem to contradict what you would like to believe. Live up to your name 'Root-stump,' and put down deep roots. Don't let your whims lead you astray."

Xat pushed himself to the limit, sitting in the cold water to become as strong as Blackskin. For he felt some special destiny was his. Each day he sat longer, whipped harder, and drank more devil's club juice. He tested his strength by trying to uproot old tree stumps and lifting big rocks. His hunting and fishing skills grew too, and he now added an occasional bear or seal to the smaller fish and game. The little family did not lack for food.

His biggest challenge came with Itc!, a heavy, seemingly immovable rock on the beach. Xat struggled to roll it over, imagining himself wrestling with Strength-of-the-North-Wind as Blackskin did. But he could barely budge it. One day he noticed that it was partially buried in the sand. He leaned against it with all his strength, rocking it to and fro to loosen it at the base. Then he laid his shoulder against it and pushed with all the force he could muster. His feet dug into the ground and he felt as though his legs were sending out roots to steady him. Suddenly the rock began to move. Gradually he rolled it over and with the first momentum began to roll it down to the water. He had overcome the mammoth rock.

One morning when Xat was busy with his exercise, he noticed a strange phenomenon in the sky. It looked like a giant kite with a long knotted tail floating above the beach. He called to his mother and grandmother to come outside to see it.

"Look at that strange thing in the sky," he said. As it came closer, they could see that the "tail" was really people holding on to one another by the feet.

"That looks like the people of our village," said his grandmother. By this time they could make out the men on the lower part with the women above them, but the children were still too far up for them to identify.

As the chain of people swung toward him, Xat ran to grab the lowest person. The plume tugged and tugged, but could not lift him off the ground. For Xat had dug his feet into the ground and sent out roots in all directions. His strong body was unshakable. With a forceful jerk he pulled the first man to the ground. A second jerk brought another down. Then, one by one, he pulled all the villagers down to earth. Everyone was amazed at Xat's display of superhuman strength.

"How did you get so strong, boy?" the men joked with him. But only he and his mother and grandmother knew of his root power, which had come to him from the roots his mother swallowed.

The rescued villagers were delighted to be home and ran to see their houses. Everything was just as they had left it. Xat and his mother and grandmother were also pleased to have their relatives back. Xat became the new chief and was highly respected for his strength and judgment at home and throughout all the villages, as word spread of his great accomplishment.

OWL WOMAN

A young woman, the wife of a high-caste man, did not get along with her mother-in-law. As was the custom, the young couple lived with the husband's parents in a screened-off section of the clan house, which they shared with other close relatives. Before her marriage, as the daughter of the chief and her father's darling, the young wife had been given whatever she wished and had had her own way in almost everything. Spirited and strong-willed, the wife resented having to defer to the wishes of her mother-in-law, mistress of the house.

Her husband, highly regarded in his own village for his hunting and fishing prowess, had won her hand with his wealth and position. At first he was delighted with his prize, finding his wife's high spirits and saucy manner amusing. So he, too, indulged her whenever possible. But when she made no attempt to adjust to the household hierarchy and submit to her mother-in-law's authority, friction arose between the two women. She avoided her husband's mother as much as possible and behaved rudely when addressed by her. Eventually her behavior was brought to the attention of her doting husband, who at last was compelled to speak with her.

"Why are you so cross with my mother?" the husband asked, in an attempt at peacemaking.

"I can't stand her bossiness," she answered with a toss of her head. "Nobody has ordered me around like this before, and I don't like it."

"Try to hide your feelings and be a little patient," he pleaded. "Somebody has to run the house or there would be chaos. My brothers' wives get along with her."

"They think she's a tyrant, too. They're just afraid to stand up to her."

"Well, she's in charge. Can't you at least try to tolerate her?" But the wife continued to play the spoiled child, and the husband, who had at first thought her edginess was due to coming into a new household, began to find her behavior trying.

The mother-in-law, who reveled in her authority, was

not blameless. Early on she sensed her daughter-in-law's hostility toward her and saw a challenge in it.

"I'll get that little lady into line in short order," she vowed, and took every opportunity to do so. First there was the episode of the fish. A load of salmon came in just as the young wives were leaving to pick berries.

"You will have to stay to help fillet and preserve the fish," she told the young wife.

"Why me?" she asked.

"Your husband's boat brought it in."

"It can wait until evening," she snapped, not missing her step with the others heading for the woods.

"Not in this heat. The men were detained two days by rough water, and the fish need attention right away."

"Come, my wife, and prepare our fish," her husband said, embarrassed at what he saw as her shirking her duties. At his stern tone, she turned back.

"Shall we stay and help?" one sister-in-law asked.

"No, you go pick berries," the young wife answered — no use turning the other women against her, too. She went over to the baskets of fish and, under the older woman's gloating eye, set about filleting her husband's catch. Ordinarily she gloried in being the wife of the man who was able to provide the village with greatly needed fish. But this time her joy had been squelched.

It was not accidental that her husband provided more fish, meat or furs than the other men. As a young man he had followed the tribal ritual of bathing, fasting, and taking devil's club juice to instill the proper attitude for receiving his uncle's special weasel spirit. That spirit had come to him when he had first reached manhood. He had fasted for eight days in the woods in an area where weasels were known to

109

live. On the last day of his fast, he came upon a huge weasel sitting on a log and cracking a small crab he had brought up from the water. The man stopped short, never having seen such a large weasel. The weasel turned and looked at him. Their eyes met and locked. First the young man was seized with a dizziness. Then a feeling of euphoria came over him as the weasel looked away and went about its business. From that day on he felt possessed of supernatural powers. He could sense when it was about to rain or when the weather would be crisp. His instincts for the feeding places of game and fish became stronger, and he was always successful at hunting or fishing. But he kept his secret to himself. At first he was pleased that he was able to delight his bride with his hunting and fishing prowess. But as time went on, her self-centered acceptance of his accomplishments saddened him.

Smaller skirmishes between the two women continued to occur, but nothing major happened for several months. Then, with the onset of winter, a woman was brought in to make fur robes for the wives of all of the sons. Again it was the young woman's husband who had supplied most of the marten and even one white sea otter. Ecstatic, the young wife wrapped herself in the otter and paraded before her husband.

"I will be stunning in a long white otter robe," she said. But her mother-in-law had other ideas.

"All the robes will be made of marten," she ordered the seamstress. "And all will be trimmed in otter."

"But the sea otter is mine!" the young woman wailed. "My husband brought it for me."

"Why should your robe be finer than those of my other sons' wives? All should be the same. By itself, the white otter pelt will make only one robe, but it's enough to trim all of them."

The vain young woman could see from her sisters-in-law's faces that they agreed with the mother-in-law. She also noticed her husband's displeased look. So she let the matter drop, and the otter was shared.

As time passed, the hostility between the two women was kept in check. Finding herself outmaneuvered, the young wife appeared submissive, resisting only occasionally. The mother-in-law, on the other hand, was growing older and was too much troubled with her own aches and pains to look for arguments with her daughter-in-law.

But the passage of time did not lessen the young woman's spirit or her resourcefulness — or her self-interest. On her own, she had devised an ingenious way of catching large amounts of herring. With strings of red cedar bark she wove hemlock boughs together to make a kind of apron, which she tied around her waist. Then she went out to a flat rock that was out of water at low tide and sat on it, letting the apron fall around the base of the rock. When the tide came in, the herring came with it and swam among the branches. As fish collected in her apron, the young woman threw them up onto the beach. Then she took them to the house and cooked them for her dinner, never sharing them with her in-laws. She did this every day during the herring season, carefully putting her apron away each time when she reached the house.

One day her ailing mother-in-law heard her cooking the herring.

"What is that you are cooking, my son's wife?"

"Oh, just some clams I collected on the beach."

"I would like some. I am hungry," she said in her still-imperious manner. The daughter-in-law bent over the fire **111** dutifully as though to pick up a roasting clam with her cooking tool, but she took a hot rock instead and dropped it into her mother-in-law's outstretched hand.

"That's hot!" she cried, dropping it onto the ground. "You have burned my hand." Then she realized that what she had dropped was no clam.

"A rock! You put a hot rock in my hand! You wicked woman! Wait until my son hears of this." Then the old woman hurried about showing her burn to the other women.

"What a cruel thing to do," crooned one. "That girl has a mean streak."

"How selfish not to give you a taste of the fish. She has always thought only of herself," another said.

"She does think she is a little better than the rest of us," a third added.

By the time her husband arrived home from hunting, a crowd of sympathizers had gathered around the mother, and they wasted no time telling him of the incident. Then his mother showed him her hand.

"See what your wife has done? She has burned my hand with a hot rock."

"A hot rock? How? Why?"

"I asked for some of the fish she was cooking. She said they were clams, but they smelled like fish."

"What kind of fish? Where would she get fish?" the son asked.

"I don't know. But every morning after you leave she goes off somewhere and does not return until late afternoon."

"We see her heading toward Herring Rock sometimes," one of the women volunteered. "She likes to be by herself."

The husband's anger grew with each revelation. This wife of his was becoming a real embarrassment. Many times she had been ill-natured toward him, accusing him of siding with his mother in their disagreements. More than once his friends had made remarks suggesting he could not control her. He had spoken sharply to her on one or two recent occasions and thought the situation had improved. But this outbreak was worse than anything that had happened so far, and the women were angry that his wife had treated his mother badly.

"I will take care of this matter when I get back," he told the women. "Now my brother and I must unload our deer and return to the hunting grounds."

As he went back to the boat, he thought about the incident, saying to himself, "I must deal more severely with my wife. Her behavior is becoming a real problem. But first I had better see what she is up to on those mysterious trips."

Several men followed him down to help unload the game.

"Where did you find all these deer?" one asked. "We hunted all morning and found nothing."

"Your hunting spirits must be working overtime," another joked. The husband smiled but kept silent.

When the deer had all been taken out and hung up to season, the husband and his brother set out again toward the hunting grounds. After they had gone only a short way, the husband turned the boat back toward a spot where they could see what was going on in the village. There they were able to see for themselves how the young wife put on the apron of hemlock boughs and, leaving her basket higher on the beach where the tide would not reach it, headed for the rock. They watched in amazement as she took the fish that caught in her hemlock apron and flung them onto the beach. When there were enough to fill her basket, she went ashore to collect them and headed for home.

"Let's get over there and catch a load of herring for ourselves," the husband said. "I have an idea."

When they had a full load, they headed for home and beached the boat. Then they went up to the house.

"Are you home from hunting already?" his wife asked. "The women told me you went out to get more deer after unloading your catch."

"We came upon a large run of herring and have a boatload of it down there," he told her.

"Herring!" she cried and ran down to the canoe.

"Look at all that herring!" she said, running her hands through the catch that was overflowing the canoe. She turned to get her basket, but it was not there. "My basket." She looked all around her. "I must have forgotten it in the excitement."

"Bring me my basket!" she called to the people up at the house. "I want to fill it with fish."

Again she dug her hands deeply into the herring, lifting some up to look at them more carefully. "They are so firm and fresh," she murmured. Then she noticed that nobody was coming down and called more loudly.

"Bring down my basket." But the people, annoyed at her cruelty to her mother-in-law, ignored her. Impatient, she shouted louder and louder. "Bring down my basket, my basket, my basket!" ("Wudikat, wudikat, wudikat," in Tlingit.) Still no one came. Yet she seemed unable to go up to get it herself. The fish seemed to hold her to them like a magnet.

"My basket, basket, basket," she continued to cry. Still nobody heeded her. They looked over at the women's husband.

"Let it be. Stay here," was all he said. He seemed to be muttering to himself, but they could not hear what he was saying. "Let her become an owl," he had uttered in a very low voice.

All through the night the woman stayed by the canoe and called for her basket. Toward morning the people noticed that her cries had changed.

"Wu! Wu! Wu!" She was now repeating only the first syllable of "wudikat," probably too exhausted to say the whole word. And her voice sounded strange too, like the hooting of an owl.

"Wu, wu, wu, wu," she cried over and over. Then her voice became more distant. She began to back away from the herring-filled canoe, and as she moved farther and farther, she took on the appearance of an owl. She kept calling "Wu, wu, wu," and gradually went out of sight.

The people were stunned. Had she really become an owl or did she just look like one? Would she return? Many days went by and there was no sign of her.

"He changed her into an owl," one of the old women said. "The husband. He has shaman powers, you know."

The people looked at her, perplexed. Then they thought awhile about what she had said.

"Maybe he does have some special powers," one of the men volunteered. "He has always brought in bigger loads of fish and game than the rest of us."

"He always knows the right places to go to hunt or fish," another added.

"His deceased uncle was a great shaman," the old

woman went on, encouraged by their responses. "Maybe he passed on some of his powers to his nephew." Now they were all listening to her. "The powerful weasel was one of his aides."

"The weasel!" the people exclaimed. Then they began to murmur among themselves. The weasel was a chief aide to the shaman when he needed magic or wanted to foretell the future. "Yes," they agreed, "the weasel's power could have changed the man's wife into an owl."

So they took the owl for their crest and raised a pole in its honor. At the top they carved an owl and at the base a weasel.

"The owl can predict bad weather," they said, assuming that it got that power from the weasel. "And we can understand it because it was once a woman."

From that time on when a young girl behaved selfishly, people would say to her, "When you get married, you will put a hot rock into your mother-in-law's hand, and for punishment you will be turned into an owl."

THE LOVE CHARM

A high-caste young man of the Raven tribe had become quite wealthy through his exceptional hunting and fishing skills and was ready to take a wife. He would have to choose a wife from the Eagles, for members did not marry within the tribe. He had noticed a girl in the village, an Eagle, who was quite beautiful and behaved in a refined manner, and he felt she would make him a fine wife. He sought out his mother's eldest brother, since it was the custom for this uncle to present the nephew's offer of marriage to the girl's parents, and told him of his wishes. But the uncle had other plans for him.

"Your mother and I thought the daughter of our brother who lives in the next village would be a better choice," he said. "Our brother is growing old and will be choosing one of his nephews to succeed him as chief. Your chances are good, since you have shown leadership qualities and prowess as a hunter and fisherman. But being married to his daughter will make them even better." Marriages were often arranged to strengthen family lineage and social standing as well as to benefit individuals. This brother, who was very rich and enjoyed high social status, would pass on his wealth and position to one of his sister's sons whom he chose to follow him as chief. His own sons would have to compete with the sons of his wife's sisters if one of their brothers was a chief.

The young man was persuaded to seek the hand of the chief's daughter. She was not considered related to him, since she was an Eagle like her mother, while the young man, like his mother and the girl's father, was a Raven. Children always belonged to their mother's tribe and were not considered related to their father's relatives.

In making the match, the young man's uncle presented the chief with many blankets and copper shields. The offer of marriage was accepted. It was also understood that the young man would succeed his father-in-law as chief. While the uncle was making the marriage arrangements, the daughter and her friends were discussing the proposal.

"Will you marry him if your parents agree?" asked one girl.

"What else can I do? He is an honorable man and will make a good chief," she answered.

"But you love somebody else."

"Yes," she sighed, thinking of the easy-going young man who had won her heart. They had not spoken to each other, of course, for young women were not allowed to speak with men before marriage, but they had ways of signaling favorites with glances and smiles. She knew her parents would never accept that man, however. The man who married her was going to succeed her father as chief. He would have to be of high caste and have high status in the community. His hunting and fishing skills would have to be outstanding, and he would have to show leadership ability. The young man she felt attracted to had good looks and charm, but not the qualities of a chief. When her parents told her of the marriage arrangement, she agreed to their wishes, and a wedding date was set.

On the appointed day the relatives gathered in the chief's house for the wedding ceremony. The young man, arrayed in a marten robe and decorated with abalone shells, came to claim his bride. Although his uncle had already compensated the family generously with blankets and copper shields, the bridegroom brought additional gifts of jewelry for the bride and carved boxes for her family. When the traditional songs were sung to lure the bride out of hiding, she appeared in the marten robe her aunt had fashioned for her.

As they made their promises to each other before the guests, the groom reached for the bride's hand. She still did not reveal her face to him, but kept it hidden in her robe.

He was puzzled. Could she be embarrassed? Or afraid? After all, taking a husband was a big step for a young girl.

"Come, my wife. You will get over your shyness in a while," he said. It did not occur to him that she might be in love with another man. The reticent bride went with her husband to their own house in her father's village, hoping that in time being the wife of the chief's successor would make her happy.

Although the ceremony to make him the chief was at least a year away, just being named the successor gained the bridegroom power as well as social position for him and his wife. Already some preparations for that day were under way. An artist had been engaged to carve the family crest on the headpiece the young man would be entitled to wear after his succession. Many women were busy sewing his robe, which would also be embellished with family crests. Plans were fermenting for the potlatch: wealth was accumulated and songs and dances were practiced. All these things were being done in anticipation of the moment when his uncle would put his hands in front of the nephew's face, give him his new name, and proclaim him chief.

But these activities did little to cheer the bride. The young man showered her with gifts and attention to win some show of affection. She warmed toward him a little the first few nights. After all, he was handsome and strong. But something seemed to be lacking in their marriage. Wasn't a new bride supposed to wait eagerly for her husband's return at the end of the day? She had noticed other brides counting off the hours, but she didn't share their excitement. Her husband was a good man and a fine provider, but she felt no thrill at the thought of seeing him soon again. Instead she went rather listlessly about her work. Her mind strayed to the charming young man and the pleasant feelings she used to have whenever their glances met. Maybe he could have made her happy.

Suddenly the bride began to feel a great longing for her family and the house she had grown up in. She would go back to them. Would her return disgrace the family? Perhaps. But her father could fix it. After all, he was chief and she was his favorite daughter.

That evening the husband returned from fishing to an empty house.

"Where is my wife?" he asked the servant.

"I think she went to visit her family," she answered. The young man sat down to eat and then went in search of his wife.

"Our daughter grew lonely for her mother and aunt and all her cousins," the girl's father explained. Not wishing to create tension between the two families, the young man did not exact the gifts due him for the girl's indiscretion. Instead he patiently persuaded his wife to return with him.

The bride took up her wifely duties and seemed content for a few weeks. But then the boredom and loneliness returned, and she was off to her father's house again.

As he went a second time to bring her back, the husband sensed a few snickers among the villagers. Nor did his cousins miss the chance to needle him.

"What's the matter, kid? Is she too much for you?" He took their ribbing good-naturedly, but was losing patience with the girl. Twice now he had been humiliated before the whole village.

"That's your problem," his father-in-law said when the bridegroom spoke to him of his wife's behavior. "You are a strong young man. You should be able to control your wife."

The groom tried to gain his wife's favor by telling her how proud he was to have her as head of the household.

"You are privileged, too, to be the wife of one who will be chief." He won a promise from her to stay with him and do her duties. But it was not long before she was off again.

Now the husband was desperate. He was in danger of losing his standing in the village, of being ridiculed. What should he do? Then one of the servants told him about the woman with the love charms.

"She's a very large woman who lives in the next village," she told him. "She has medicine to get your wife to love you. Her father was a shaman, and she learned this craft from him."

"Love medicine? But does it work?" he asked. He had heard of herbs to cure illnesses. And he had heard the hunters talk of "glare" medicine to make sighted game become dizzy and easy to capture. There was even a medicine to capture game that had escaped. These medicines were dispensed by shamans or those to whom they entrusted their secrets.

"The love charm has worked for some girls," she assured him. "Haven't you heard of medicine that makes you happy or that makes you popular? Some chiefs use that when they give potlatches so everybody will admire them."

"Like medicines that take away your strength or make you a good marksman?" he asked. "But I did not know there was a love medicine. Tell me how to find this woman."

He listened to all the servant could tell him. Then in the morning he set out with gifts and four companions for the next village. They arrived by early evening and had **122** no trouble getting directions to the woman's place. Her people received them graciously and invited them to share their meal.

Seated in the place of honor was an immensely heavy woman who was being ministered to by several servants. She was dining on large portions of the finest cuts of venison and salmon served out of elaborately carved wooden bowls. A carved dish in the shape of a seal, its rim inlaid with abalone shells, held eulachon oil, and from another bowl in the shape of a wolf, berries were being ladled with an intricately carved wooden spoon. The woman nodded when introduced to the men, but no discussion of their mission was allowed until the meal was finished. Then, after she learned the nature of their visit, she ordered preparations for her purifying bath before giving advice.

The servants brought in logs to revive the fire to heat the bath water. While they filled the tub, the rejected husband looked with apprehension at the huge woman. Her round face was circled with extra chins, and the skin was smoothed tightly across it. Above the elbow, her large arms looked like hams. As she lifted them, the great folds of flesh swayed loosely. When the servants helped her to get up and go behind the screen to bathe, she moved her enormous body wth difficulty. Her servants would be able to wash only one leg at a time, as each leg was bigger than a large child.

After her bath she returned to her place by the fire and listened to the young man's request. Her forbidding mien softened as she looked at the handsome and superbly fit young man before her. While he told of his love for his wife and his attentions to her, the woman's eyes misted and her expression seemed almost sensuous.

"I know about love," she told him. "I have borne **123**

my husband many children."

"I am a very rich man and the leader of my people," he explained. "Yet I am having trouble with my wife, whom I have showered with much love and many gifts. She keeps running away. As you can see, I am strong and in good condition, since I exercise and bathe each morning. I have been told there is a charm that can attract my wife's love."

"Yes, there is a plant that will help you," she said.

"I have brought gifts for you if you are able to help me," he said, motioning to one of his companions to offer them. She held up a gleaming necklace of twisted copper and then fingered an intricately carved wooden comb for her hair. These would be fine additions to her collection of gifts brought by previous petitioners. Two such gifts she was wearing now. Around her neck hung a necklace of charms carved from dentalia, which rested on her ample breast, and a delicately worked copper bracelet circled her huge wrist. She found his offers acceptable and decided to advise him.

"The plant you need is the starflower that blooms in June and has roots that look like a little man. You must be careful in uprooting it, though. Gather the plant before dawn, before the raven calls. You need not speak to the plant or leave a gift in its place," she went on. "But wrap it in a piece of your clothing, along with something of your wife's. Then replant it. And be sure not to keep it out of the ground for more than one day." Then she gave him an eagle's tail with a red streak of paint across it.

"Go to your father's village and take this eagle's tail with you. Around the point there, you will see some land otters coming up from the water. Look carefully for the white one. When you see her step up on the beach, raise your eagle's tail and see whether she will stand still. If she does so and does not run away, go right by her without touching her. Then return to your father-in-law's village. Your wife will come directly to you."

Though he thought the instructions bizarre, the young man carried them out to the letter. That night he and his four companions went to bed early, and then just before dawn they set out in search of the delicate starflower. In the faint predawn light before the raven's call, they found a starflower. The husband wrapped it carefully in his skin cape, as the woman had directed, adding the lock of his wife's hair he always kept with him, and then he replanted it. After sunrise he carried out the woman's instructions with the land otters. The white one appeared and stood still as he waved the eagle's tail, and he passed by without touching her.

The next day the men returned to the village of his wife's family, and he went to her father's house to find her. As she saw him approaching, the girl began to feel a strong inclination toward her husband. The closer he came, the more powerful became the attraction. Finally she threw her arms around him and help him tightly.

At first the husband was happy with the success of the love charm. His wife was really affectionate now. But then he noticed he was not feeling the same delight. He no longer felt the affection of their early marriage. His love for her had cooled. Did his state have anything to do with the starflower? The astoundingly fat lady surely would have warned him if it would affect his own ardor. Or was it the many humiliations at his wife's hands that had dampened his feelings for her?

"Stay here at your father's house a while longer," he said to her. "I have work I must do."

He returned to his father's village to think. As he approached his father's house, he saw the pretty girl of the Eagle tribe, to whom he had been attracted before his marriage. She smiled at him, and the old longings returned.

"I wish I had that starflower now," he thought. He had replanted it right away as the large woman had instructed. "But it probably would not work on a different woman."

To his surprise, the young girl seemed just as strongly attracted to him. Was the potion still working? If so, why was it working for her but not the other girls? Of course, he had not looked at them with the same longing.

"This is the woman I should have married," he finally realized. "We have always had a warm feeling for each other. Maybe the charm is working for us because of this natural attraction."

Then he said to his companions, "Since my wife does not love me, I will let her go back to her family. Then I will ask for this woman's hand in marriage."

"You are a very eligible man — chief material," one of them replied. "A good provider with a high-caste lineage."

The young woman was from a high-born family, too, and conducted herself well. She would make a good wife. But did he dare tell his father he wanted to relinquish his first wife and the position of chief that went with her?

Again, he need not have worried. Word of his fickle wife's behavior had already surfaced in the village. "You have suffered enough humiliation at their hands," his father said. "There is no need to return to that village."

Before making an offer of marriage to the second young woman, the young man had to divorce his first wife. Since she had deserted him, it was really up to her family to make amends by returning all of his gifts and making additional ones to compensate for the humiliation caused him and his family. But he wanted no hard feelings between the two families. Nor did he want any harm to come to the new wife. So he let the first wife's family keep the things he had already given and sent them additional generous gifts of slaves and property. These actions seemed to satisfy the honor of the first wife's family.

But her family was not so forgiving of the rejected wife, who had nearly caused hostilities between the two families. Though her parents still loved her dearly, other relatives treated her coolly. They felt she had brought them disgrace.

Now she realized she had been foolish to think that her father as chief could make everything right if she just went home. "I have acted like a child in refusing to take the responsibilities of a wife," she told herself. "Now I have thrown away the chance of being married to a chief."

At least she had not been unfaithful to her husband; the tribal code dictated a severe punishment for that. But she had relinquished the position that came with being married into a family of such high status. As it was, she was forced to live humbly with her family until another husband, probably of lower status, might come forward. Her fickleness had cost her social position and the love of the man now made dear to her by the magic charm.

ABOUT THE AUTHOR

Mary L. Beck is a classical scholar (M.A. from Stanford) who has lived in Ketchikan, Alaska, since 1951, when she married a third-generation Alaskan. Besides rearing a family, she taught literature and writing courses for thirty years at Ketchikan Community College, a branch of the University of Alaska. Mary has an abiding interest in the Native culture of Southeast Alaska and a commitment to recording its oral literature. Previous works include a book, *Heroes and Heroines in Tlingit-Haida Legend*, and articles on Native mythology and on travel by small boat to towns and Native communities in Southeast Alaska.

ABOUT THE ILLUSTRATOR

Marvin Oliver is an internationally acclaimed contemporary Native American artist who works in metal, glass, wood, and on paper. He teaches Pacific Northwest Coast Indian art at the University of Washington and at the University of Alaska Ketchikan. He is a Seattle resident.